Writing

FOR CHILDREN

Books in the 'Writing Handbooks' series

Developing Characters for Script Writing • Rib Davis
Freelance Copywriting • Diana Wimbs
Freelance Writing for Newspapers • Jill Dick
Ghostwriting • Andrew Crofts
Marketing Your Book: An Author's Guide • Alison Baverstock
Writing Biography & Autobiography • Brian D. Osborne
Writing Comedy • John Byrne
Writing Crime Fiction • H.R.F. Keating
Writing Dialogue for Scripts • Rib Davis
Writing Fantasy and Science Fiction • Lisa Tuttle
Writing for Magazines • Jill Dick
Writing a Play • Steve Gooch
Writing Poetry • John Whitworth
Writing Popular Fiction • Rona Randall
Writing Romantic Fiction • Daphne Clair and Robyn Donald
Writing Sitcoms • John Byrne and Marcus Powell
Writing for Soaps • Chris Curry
Writing Successful Textbooks • Anthony Haynes
Writing for Television • Gerald Kelsey
Writing a Thriller • André Jute

Other books for writers

Novel Writing • Evan Marshall
The Reader's Encyclopedia • William Rose Benét
Research for Writers • Ann Hoffmann
The Weekend Novelist • Robert J. Ray and Bret Norris
Word Power: A Guide to Creative Writing • Julian Birkett
Writers' and Artists' Yearbook
Children's Writers' and Artists' Yearbook

WRITING HANDBOOKS

Writing

FOR CHILDREN

LINDA STRACHAN

A & C Black • London

Dedicated to
The Scattered Authors' Society
(The 'other' SAS)

1 3 5 7 9 10 8 6 4 2

A & C Black Publishers Limited
38 Soho Square
London W1D 3HB
www.acblack.com

ISBN 978–07136–8774–3

First published 2008

A CIP catalogue record for this book is
available from the British Library

This book is produced using paper made from wood grown in
managed, sustainable forests. It is natural, renewable and recyclable.
The logging and manufacturing processes conform to the
environmental regulations of the country of origin.

Printed in the UK by Caligraving Ltd, Thetford, Norfolk

Contents

Section 3 – Submissions to a Publisher or Agent

Section 4 – Now You Are Published

Section 5 – Useful Information

Introduction

Writing for children: What makes it special?

The audience is more honest, and more demanding. They won't be patronised, and they won't flatter. They won't be impressed if you try to show off. But if you love your readers, you can forge a relationship of pure honest joy.

Eleanor Updale

Children are constantly learning how to make sense of the world around them, and books play a significant part in that process. They require a wide range of books depending on their age, their ability to read and understand, and their particular interests – but first they have to learn what a story is and then how to read themselves. Children progress from simple stories with lots of illustrations to easy readers and progressively on to more complex stories and texts. They may want to read poetry or non-fiction, and they need books that are specifically written to meet the demands of teachers for use in schools. These represent some of the many markets open to children's writers.

Writing for children can and should be enormous fun, but don't let that fool you: children's books are often more challenging and more complex than they may at first seem. Writing is hard work, and it's not any easier because the readers are children. It can also be extremely rewarding, but not necessarily in monetary terms. Surprisingly few children's writers can survive on their advances and royalties alone.

When you say 'I'm a children's writer' people often assume that you write for tiny tots, as if children weren't of all ages. They seldom ask, 'What age of children?'

Catherine MacPhail

Saying that you want to write for children is all very well, but you have to consider what age of child you are most comfortable writing for, and what kind of book would interest children of that age. To decide this, and indeed if you are serious about writing for children at all, the best single piece of advice I've ever come across is to read as many children's books as you can. All the children's writers I know read a lot of children's books.

Read, read, read; write, write, write.   **Julia Jarman**

Spend time in your local library or in a bookshop with a good children's department, and find out what has been published for children in the last couple of years. Then, read as much of it as you can. Get to know what is new; what books children of different ages are reading; and what is selling and winning prizes – especially those for competitions that are judged by children. Just because you were once a child who loved reading does not mean that you will automatically be familiar with children's reading tastes today. Listen to children's writers speaking at festivals, and ask your local children's bookseller or youth librarian their opinion of the best of recently published books. They usually have a wealth of knowledge about what is being published and what is being bought and borrowed.

I love writing for children because you can invent a world of your own. It's similar to going on holiday, only better because all your characters are waiting for you like old friends!

Elizabeth Kay

In every area of work there is a period of apprenticeship during which you learn from the best practitioners. Writing for children is no different. It requires a love of books, particularly children's books; stamina and determination; and a fairly thick skin to enable you to withstand the knocks and rejections that may come your way. But despite all the hard work and difficulties, most children's writers wouldn't want to do anything else.

> One of the best things is being paid to daydream and follow your imagination. Being able to do this anywhere – in my favourite coffee shop, in the park on a sunny morning, halfway up a mountain. Creeping out of bed when everyone else is asleep because a great idea has hit you.   **Julie Bertagna**

About this book

This book is about capturing the wonder that children feel at the simplest things, and translating that fresh, original way of looking at the world into new and exciting stories that they will enjoy reading.

It focuses on writing for younger children up to about 10–12 years, and although some of the general information applies equally to writing teenage and Young Adult (YA) books, these are areas that have their own set of challenges and criteria which cannot fully be addressed here.

The book is divided into five sections, as follows:

1. Different kinds of writing for children
There are many different markets and opportunities for children's writers. Discover what kind of books you want to write, and explore some writing styles you may not previously have considered.

2. A writer's toolkit
Learn about creating believable characters, dialogue, plotting, beginnings and endings and some of the other skills you need to write well. There are exercises designed to help you identify your strengths and weaknesses and to give you an opportunity to practise. (This is more of a taster than a full writing course, but it will get you started.)

3. Preparing your manuscript
How to present your work to a publisher, including writing a cover letter and a synopsis. Find out the difference between vanity publishing, self-publishing and Print on Demand.

4. Now you are published ...
Many new writers think that once they have a contract with a publisher, it's all sorted. In fact, that is only the beginning. What can you expect going forwards? How best to organise your time and finances? How should you prepare for the public side of being a writer – for example, for school and library visits and other public events? Here you will find some helpful tips and guidelines.

5. Useful information
This section includes a glossary of terms; lists of useful organisations and websites where you can find out about prizes and bursaries and other information for writers; information on writing courses, writers' groups and writers' magazines; and details of the writers who have contributed to this book.

Section 1
Different Kinds of Writing
for Children

1.

Different Ages, Different Markets

A good children's book is accessible and thought-provoking, and sometimes a good children's book is just a lot of fun. I like writing children's books because I like stories.

Catherine Johnson

One of the most exciting things about writing for children is the sheer diversity. You have different ages to choose from; you can write picture books, easy readers, short books for more confident readers, or novels – each quite different in length and often in content. When making your choice there are other considerations, too. Do you want to write for the educational market – books written for use in schools – or would you rather write poetry or plays, a series or a 'stand alone', or perhaps a picture book for the very young?

Many children's authors write consistently for the same genre or age group, while others write across the board. Either is acceptable, and this is another reason why it's an advantage to write for children. It's always a challenge to try something different; you never know what skills you might have if you don't try. However, you should always write about things that fascinate or excite you. If your subject matter doesn't touch *you*, the writer, how can you expect it to appeal to others?

Genre

Whether it is adventure, crime, realism, humour, science fiction or fantasy, choose a genre that excites you as a writer. Don't base your decision on what you have heard is the latest fad in publishing, the latest in a line of bestsellers or the 'only' thing children are reading: such considerations are pointless. By the time you have written your book and submitted it to a publisher, the fashion will probably have changed, the publishers will be looking for something else and the press will have latched on to another 'phenomenon'.

The most important thing is to write well and to be true to the story. If you love fantasy then try and find a way to write fantasy that is different from all the rest. Make it your own and original, but don't make it so obscure that no one can understand it, just because you are trying to be different.

If you prefer to write humorously, or to create exciting, spooky or perhaps serious or realistic stories, don't let the latest fads either entice you or put you off. If your writing and your story are good enough, your work will be taken up despite the latest trend. You may even start a trend of your own!

Your choice of genre depends on your own taste, but whatever that may be, you must make your writing exciting and interesting; it should be full of action and page-turning events. Keep children at the heart of the story, don't be tempted to cheat the reader with an easy or illogical ending, and you will have a success on your hands.

Political correctness or being 'PC'

We live in a society that is becoming increasingly concerned with political correctness. Sometimes we are so careful not to offend anyone that this can be taken to ridiculous extremes. But it is also important to remember that there are good reasons for being inclusive. As writers, we should adopt and encourage a balanced approach, and at the very least recognise the variety of experiences and cultures that children have to understand and cope with.

> All children need to recognise themselves somewhere in the world around them.   **Penny Dolan**

If you want your work to be accepted for publication, you have to be aware that there are some things you cannot do. Different rules may apply according to such things as the age of your reader; whether your book will be used in schools as a textbook, and therefore is 'required' reading matter; or if it's a question of the parent or the child choosing whether or not to buy your book. There are some things that publishers will not publish – often because they are making a commercial rather than a moral judgement. Why would they publish something that no one will buy? For the writer, then, a common sense approach is probably best. If something risks being contentious but you are very keen to write it, speak to an editor or agent first and ask whether the subject matter and/or the approach is likely to be acceptable or if it will cause a problem. If the answer is the latter, at that point you have to decide whether you feel it's worth pursuing.

No one is going to want to publish a children's book that glorifies or encourages dangerous behaviour, or anything that promotes bullying or other antisocial activity. That is not to say you can't tackle these subjects within the context of a story; in fact, they may be welcomed as long as they are skilfully handled. The problem occurs if your characters are seen to be benefiting from crime or bad behaviour, or if your readers are thought likely to want to copy it because it is portrayed as aspirational. If you do choose to address such issues, the way in which you end your story is especially important. Make sure there is some kind of resolution and consequence to antisocial, stupid or dangerous behaviour, so that the reader is left in no doubt that it is not without penalty. However, you need to avoid preaching or being dictatorial, so that you don't alienate your reader.

In the field of educational publishing, there are certain subjects that publishers will not be keen on at all. To be safe, always check with them. If your book is to be published in other countries, publishers may have additional reasons to avoid certain subject matter: perhaps there are local sensitivities which may cause it to be rejected. You may be asked to change some passages for that reason; try not to take this personally or feel that the publisher is being unreasonable. Their reasons will usually be clear and almost universally to the benefit of sales, so complaining that they don't see your point of view is irrelevant and pointless; you are unlikely to change their opinion.

Don't be boring!

Never be boring; children have a built-in 'boring!' detector. Not only will they not put up with a boring book, they will tell their friends. On the flip side, if they enjoy a book then they will be happy to tell the world. Children enjoy different types of books and so much of the difference between great and boring lies in the way in which you tell the story. Always look for freshness and immediacy in your writing.

> Why do I write children's books? The answer is 'in response to a challenge'. Mind you, I quickly found – and still do – that writing children's books is very enjoyable.
>
> **Alan Cliff**

In this section, we'll look at some of the different areas of writing for children that you might want to try.

2.

Picture Books

Picture books are like poetry. Tell the story with as few words as possible. Every word needs to be perfect. Every word needs to earn its keep.   **Malachy Doyle**

What is a picture book?

A picture book looks very simple; just a few words and a lot of lovely images. Its very simplicity is deceiving. The most successful picture books are often quite complex when you analyse the actual content.

One of my favourite picture books is *The Man on the Moon* by Simon Bartram. On the surface it seems quite simple: it tells the story of Bob, whose job it is to go to the moon every day and get it ready for tourists. He then tidies up afterwards before he returns home to Earth. There is a lovely subtext carried in the illustrations, because as he goes about his everyday tasks the Man on the Moon tells the reader frequently and positively that there are no such things as aliens. Meanwhile, behind him on the moon and in silhouette on the buses back on earth we can see little green aliens. Children love humour and often catch on very quickly to this kind of thing. Such sub-plots and layers make a picture book fun to read again and again.

Picture books vary in style and size. You could call a 'board book' – a book made of solid board or very thick pages for babies and very young children – a picture book. With little or no words these can vary from 3–4 pages to slightly longer, and can comprise only pictures or just a few words. It's strange to think that you can be the author of a book that has no words, but in essence you still have to create the story.

Usually a picture book has either more pictures than words or is at least around 50 per cent pictures. The maximum word count for a picture book is around 1000 words. There are some short picture-book texts, such as Malachy Doyle's *The Dancing Tiger*, which uses rhyme and is around 200 words in total – varying between five and 25 words on each double-page spread. There are also longer picture books, such as my version of the 'Greyfriar's Bobby' story; this has around 2500 words with between 100 and 200 words on a double-page spread.

Although the majority of picture books are standalone titles, some have sequels, such as *The Gruffalo* and *The Gruffalo's Child*, or a series such as my Hamish McHaggis series, which currently extends to seven storybooks with the potential for more to come. One favourite when my children were babies was a series of board books called *Find the Duck*, *Find the Puppy*, etc., which had no words at all.

Picture books are usually written for the 0–3 and 3–5 age groups.

Above all, a picture book needs a good strong story. There may be few words, but each one should be chosen with particular care. Because these stories are aimed at a very young age group, the story must be told clearly and simply.

Normally a picture book will have 12 double-page spreads. It is important to tell your story evenly over the pages, taking the story-arc to a climax about three-quarters of the way through. The resolution should then follow. This means that you have to pace your story over the pages, making sure it doesn't come to an end after, say, only 7–8 spreads. I find it useful, once I have a storyline, to look at how it would stretch over 12 spreads, using a page marked into 12 boxes, with a fine line marking the middle of the page. This helps me visualise the book and see how the action flows.

Who buys a picture book?

One thing that makes a picture book different is that it must appeal to 'layers' of adults before it ever gets anywhere near a child: the editor, who will decide whether to publish it; the bookseller, who decides whether to stock it in the bookshop; and finally the adult, who will buy the book for a child.

So keep in mind that although your picture book must delight and appeal to the child it is bought for, it should be exciting enough to interest and delight the adults who find it first. Achieve this, and you will have a success on your hands.

What about the pictures?

When writing a picture book it helps if you have a good sense of visualisation. You need to be able to see in your mind the pictures that might go with your text, even if, when the book has been illustrated, the pictures may bear little or no resemblance to your original ideas.

> Good picture-book texts are as much about what is unsaid as what is said. Much of the setting, characterisation, the humour and the action will be covered in the illustrations.
>
> **Malachy Doyle**

You should try to keep in mind that the pictures will carry some of the story, particularly if your story is told in a shorter number of words. I usually have a mental image of the book as if it were in front of me, fully illustrated, as I mould the text.

If you are able to draw, you might be tempted to do your own illustrations. However, unless you are trained in illustration or have a high level of artistic skill, don't do it. One very good reason for this is that editors who receive pictures and text together are sometimes in a dilemma, especially if they love the text and feel that the illustrations are either not up to standard or equally are just not right for the market. They may want the text but not the illustrations, or the other way around.

This also applies if you have a friend who illustrates and you send in your text and their illustrations. You don't want the publisher to reject the entire package rather than get into a discussion about using the text or pictures separately. It would be better for your illustrator friend to send in samples of their work independently. If their illustrations are good enough, the editor will then try to marry their style to a text which they think would suit that particular type of illustration and the market it's aimed at.

There is another reason why you should avoid illustrating your own text – one that becomes clear when you consider the thought-processes behind commissioning a picture book from the editor's point of view.

The commercial risks associated with publishing a picture book are huge, and this naturally makes publishers wary. If you are a new author – one whose name the public, the bookshop buyer or the foreign-rights buyer will not recognise as a successful picture-book author – the publisher may want to team you up with an established illustrator who has a good track record in the field. Sometimes, of course, this works the other way around: a new illustrator will be teamed up with an established author.

It is very expensive to print full-colour picture books, even in these days of amazing print technology. Publishers therefore want some security that they will get enough sales to make the undertaking viable in a very competitive market.

The words

When you write a picture book, remember that it's intended to be read out loud to a child. This means that the vocabulary you use does not have to be restricted to words the child would be able to read, and that you can use some words that the child might not understand. However, make sure that your choice of words does not detract from the flow or interrupt the story, or worse, become wordy. Avoid words that would be too technical or obscure for a child to guess from the pictures or the sense of the story. Often the pictures, and the context in which the words are used, will help the child understand any words that might otherwise be confusing.

Textural language is wonderful in a picture book, but bear in mind that sometimes less is more. Don't be afraid to edit your text – it can often improve it.

Starting out

When I was very small I discovered one day that you could tell where a person was looking by the direction in which their eyes were turning. I remember being a little embarrassed to discover that everyone else seemed to know this already. Try to look at the world with a child's innocence and wonder, and sometimes an ignorance of the things that as adults we take for granted.

> I have never forgotten the books I loved as a child. They are trapped in my head on continuous loop, along with all the other stuff of childhood: the smell of bonfire night, damp sheds and dressing-up clothes, papier mâché, paint, glue and glitter.
>
> **Nicola Browne**

When choosing your subject matter, aim for the following – all of which will feature in most good picture books:

- A story with **layers** – different layers of storyline or theme.
- **Repetition**, either of phrases or of single words, or perhaps repetition of a theme told in a slightly different way each time.
- **Rhythm** – the way the words sound as you read them. This is one of the most important things in any book designed to be read aloud. As with writing rhyme, it's easy to force the rhythm when reading your own work, so get someone else to read it aloud. You will then be free to see if the rhythm works without any strain on the part of the reader.
- A story that is **comforting**, especially at the end.
- A story that comes **full circle**. It should resolve the original problem raised at the beginning in a logical and realistic fashion, leaving the reader satisfied.

Always bear in mind that young children need reassurance, and a picture book is not the place to terrify them or leave them frightened that the world is about to crash about their ears. Some of the best picture books leave the reader with a smile, and as they are often read at bedtime this is even more important. No one wants irate parents telling you how your book left their child with nightmares! It's important to resolve problems or show how they might be resolved, and to reassure the child that there are solutions to any issues raised by the story.

A picture book also needs to leave the reader and the child with a sense of completeness. The story starts off, goes on a journey, and returns to the ending and a resolution. There are many wonderful picture books, and it's essential that you read as many as possible to get a feel for the flow of the text. Look especially at some that have been published during the last year, to see the trends that publishers are currently interested in. As with most other kinds of books, trends in picture books have changed in the last 10–15 years.

It's worth bearing in mind that if you are writing a picture-book text which deals with a theme that might be potentially frightening or worrying for a young child, it can be useful to remove the story a little from real life by making your character an animal or other type of creature. The idea of an animal in a difficult situation is less worrying to a child than the thought of a child in danger.

This technique can also be used in a story where you want to write about a child coping with a potentially difficult or danger-ous situation. In *The Gruffalo* by Julia Donaldson, a little mouse is accosted in the forest by different creatures. They all want to eat him, but he tells them he is off to meet a scary monster called the Gruffalo. When the Gruffalo itself appears and wants to eat the mouse, the clever creature turns this around by telling the Gruffalo that he (the mouse) is the scariest creature in the wood. He invites the Gruffalo to follow him and find out why. And of course the Gruffalo, walking along behind the mouse, terrifies the other creatures.

The idea of a small mouse in a scary wood is not nearly as frightening for small children as the thought of *themselves* wandering in a deep, dark forest. Removing the child from the story and placing a creature or animal as the main character gives a level of separation from reality. It also avoids any idea that the child might try something dangerous, and stops the story from becoming too frightening for an active imagination.

The Gruffalo has a repetitive theme, but because of the

wonderful use of creative vocabulary and rhyme the repetition adds to the feel of the story and to the anticipation. The picture book never becomes boring, however many times you read it; part of this is achieved by the wonderful rhythm of the rhyming text as you read it aloud.

> I think a children's writer gets much closer to their reader's heart and soul and can leave an impression for life.
>
> Nick Green

Thinking in pictures – visualisation

> Try and allow the pictures to carry some of the story. Remember that it's unnecessary to repeat something that's perfectly clear from the illustration. Ideally, the two should work together to make up the whole story. *Rosie's Walk* by Pat Hutchins is a perfect example. **Adele Geras**

I have touched on this, but it's worth repeating that once you have your idea, it can help to 'think visually'. What would the pages look like, and how much of your story can be told in the images? This allows you to concentrate on the text and avoid making it too lengthy.

One thing to remember is that although you may develop a strong idea of how your book will look, the reality is likely to be completely different. When I first had the idea for *What Colour is Love?* I imagined the illustrations as soft, lifelike watercolour images of the elephant and other animals. Then my editor suggested David Wojtowycz and showed me some of his previous illustrations. They were so different from what I'd imagined that I was completely thrown and wondered how my story would look with these bold, modern illustrations. But I trusted my editor, who I knew was very experienced, and her reasons made a lot of sense – although I must admit to being worried until I saw David's first colour roughs. They were glorious, and he had my main character, the baby elephant called 'Small Smooth and Grey', just right. I was completely won over.

One of the great things about a picture book is that it represents the collaboration of two artistic talents – the writer and the illustrator. It's a work of two halves. The illustrator can often add a completely different, and sometimes unexpected, dimension to a picture-book text. So, while it's very useful to visualise the story while you are writing it, bear in mind that the illustrator chosen for your book may have quite a different style. Their contribution to the finished result is likely to be nothing like your original, imagined version. It can be difficult at first, to let go of your story enough to accept such a radical change; but if you want to be published it's worth remembering that the editor has just as much interest in your book becoming a success as you do.

Editors are experienced in the book market, and although you should always have a discussion with them regarding anything you are unhappy about, try to understand their reasoning. If you are not prepared to accept the style of their chosen illustrator, it's up to you to say so at an early stage. And if it turns out that you can find no common ground of understanding, you may then have to consider looking for another publisher who will publish your work. There can be no guarantee that you will find one.

What to write about

> I always write picture books backwards; the ending is **so** important – so I think of the ending first, then work out how to get there.   **Vivian French**

The end of a picture book is often what will make a child want to hear the story again and again. Even if you have a good idea, it's vitally important that you know how you are going to bring the story to a complete and satisfying close.

When starting out, you might have an idea already. If not, try to think of a theme – perhaps something that is lost; a fear of the dark or of the unknown; food that a child might like or dislike; a misunderstanding of the world or of what is said by adults. When I was little I used to think the rhyme 'Twinkle, twinkle, little star' had the line 'like a tea-tray in the sky' in it. This gave me a lovely visual image of a tray with teapot, cups, saucers, sugar and milk floating overhead. When choosing your theme or images, let your imagination run wild. Listen to little children and hear what they are saying, discover what they are thinking, and listen to their misconceptions. See if any of this can be used in a story.

If you decide to use one of the more familiar themes, such as a new baby in the house or starting school or nursery, be sure to come up with an original slant. Consider telling the story from a different viewpoint; make certain that your writing is fresh and unusual. If it isn't, and you are writing about a 'well-worn' theme, you have very little chance of getting your story published. Take a thorough look at the picture books currently being published, and either choose an unusual theme or make a familiar one surprising.

As a general rule it's a good idea to keep all adult characters slightly in the background, so that the child or child-character becomes the main focus of the story all the way through. Make sure that nothing you write encourages a child to try something dangerous. If you need your child to be in a potentially difficult or dangerous situation, it's a good idea to make this happen through no conscious decision of the child. So for example, if a child gets lost, perhaps it's because they have been looking at something (possibly in a shop window) and when they look up their parent is gone. Don't have the child purposely walking away from the parent – and make sure there is a happy ending!

To rhyme or not to rhyme

When it's done really well, rhyme is wonderful to read. However, many publishers advise against it, partly because it is more difficult to secure translations and foreign rights sales if a book is in rhyme (although quite a few bestsellers do rhyme and are translated into many languages very successfully).

The most important element of any picture book is the quality of the writing. If you are genuinely able to write good rhyme without sacrificing anything in vocabulary, texture or story to make it work, then give it a go. Some picture-book authors are incredibly good at this, but most people just do not have the ability to make their text rhyme without losing something in the overall sound of the text. If you're unsure, avoid rhyme – or, use very little and if you find the story becoming at all strained, discard the rhyme but give the text a strong rhythm instead.

Whether or not your story rhymes, many writers find it easier to get it down on paper first, and then go back and refine the text – removing the odd word or reworking a phrase until they are completely happy. This is particularly important in a picture-book text, where every single word counts.

Working with an illustrator

A lot of my books have been illustrated, and they have almost all had different illustrators. When creating a picture book I have a mental image of what the pictures might look like, but this often turns out to be nothing like the finished article. This is because a picture book is very much a book of two halves – two creative people each adding their own signature to the story in words or in pictures. I normally give a short brief for the illustrator to work from, page to page; I then have some input once the first roughs are produced and a final comment before it all goes to press.

Sometimes if a book is particularly successful, a trade publisher may be keen to pair up a writer and illustrator for a second or subsequent book. This doesn't necessarily mean that they actually meet to work together; in some cases you may not meet or speak to your illustrator at all. It might come as a surprise that until I started work on the Hamish McHaggis series with Sally J Collins, I had never met or even spoken to any of the illustrators of over 40 books I had written previously.

With the Hamish McHaggis series, working so closely with the illustrator from the outset meant that from the earliest stage of creating the characters Sally and I were able to discuss what each would look like. I gave Sally an idea of their personalities and she created various different versions of the main character, Hamish McHaggis, until we both agreed that he was right.

Sally was keen to avoid dressing the animals in clothes, so we decided on accessories instead. Each character had their own 'statement': Hamish with his tartan hat, Jeannie the Osprey with her pink beads and pink painted claws, Rupert the hedgehog with his bow tie and glasses, and Angus the Pine Marten with his red cap. These items also helped to cement their personalities.

Sally and I don't always agree on everything, but we respect each other's areas of expertise and have a lot of fun. Working collaboratively does not suit everyone, but a close partnership with the right person can be an enjoyable and productive experience. You can help to further the process by giving a clear and concise illustrative brief; this may take the form of a couple of sentences or so above the text for each page, or simply some comments where you have strong feelings about what should be represented on a particular page – and how you envisage this working.

Bear in mind that when you first submit a picture-book text to an editor, you don't need to send in any accompanying images or sketches. Your text has to be good enough to excite the editor before it is illustrated. The illustrator's brief is only necessary when clarifying any specifics that are not obvious from the text – such as the aliens in *The Man on the Moon* (*see* page 6).

Summing up

To get any book published, you need not only a good idea and a story that is well written and original, but also a good dollop of luck and a lot of determination to persevere. That is particularly true about writing picture books. There are so many out there already that you have to make sure yours has something new to say and is going to have that 'Ahh!' factor that really seems to sell picture books.

There are no absolute rules for writing a picture book, but there are some generally accepted guidelines:

- A picture book usually has 12 double-page spreads but can occasionally have more.
- Content should be both sensible and sensitive. Avoid potentially contentious or upsetting themes. If your chosen story-situation may be difficult or dangerous, you would be wise to use 'non-human' characters to remove things a little from real life.
- Unless you are particularly skilled in both areas, do not send in both text and illustrations to a publisher.
- Only use rhyme if you are very confident that you can carry it off. Otherwise, focus on achieving a strong rhythm.
- Keep in mind that although your picture book must appeal to the child for whom it is bought, it should be interesting and original enough to delight the adults who find it first. Consider the reaction of editors, bookshop buyers and parents/grandparents/aunties and uncles, etc.
- The pictures often carry a lot of the story. While they may enhance it, the story must nevertheless be strong, complete and original enough without pictures to entice a publisher in the first instance.

I think a children's writer gets much closer to their reader's heart and soul and can leave an impression for life.

Nick Green

3.

Writing for 5–7, 7–9, 8–12 Years

What kind of book do you want to write, and who are you writing it for? A five year old is not going to want the same kind of story as a child aged ten or eleven; their attention span is shorter and their interests quite different.

You also need to consider the age of your main character in relation to the age of your intended reader. When writing for children, a general rule is that your characters should be a year or so older than – or at least the same age as – your target reader. Children often aspire to be like the characters in the books they enjoy, and they almost invariably wish to be a year or two older than they are; your book will therefore have more child appeal if you follow this guideline. It is particularly important not to feature main characters who are much younger than your target readership, and only on rare occasions does an adult main character work in a children's book. Some writers have been very successful with an adult main character in teenage or YA (Young Adult) books, such as Eleanor Updale's *Montmorency*, but these are the exceptions.

Age levels when stated on the back of books, in bookshops or even in publishers' briefs can be confusing. Just as children of a similar age have different tastes, abilities and experience, so this is reflected in their reading interests and abilities – which can be equally as varied. Age levels in books are just a general indication and should not be taken as hard and fast rules. Some publishers or bookshops will use the range of 6–9 years, while others specify 7–9 and/or 8–12.

Unlike adults, children require different kinds or writing depending on their age as well as their ability to read and understand. Their rate of emotional development can also vary widely, which is why there are no absolutes. Publishers, parents and bookshops all require some way of categorising children's books, so age ranges are generally used – but these are just guidelines. One eight year old may have the ability to read anything that is put in front of them, from newspapers to thick tomes, while their best friend might struggle with anything more than a comic book.

Boys versus girls?

Whatever your personal views on what children should or should not read, for good marketing reasons publishers often pitch different kinds of books to boys and to girls – especially those aged between seven and ten years. This is why you see books with pink and fluffy covers containing stories about princesses and fairies published for girls, and action adventures published for boys. Of course, there are books with plenty of action in them where the cover is pink and the main character is a girl. And perhaps this is a shame, because there is some evidence that boys would like to read these kinds of stories but are put off by the thought of being seen with a book that has a pink cover. Boys may also tend to be less interested in books where the main character is a girl – and many girls like action and adventure stories that are promoted as 'boy' books. In reality, as long as the story is gripping and exciting, it's possible for it to appeal to both sexes.

In any case, the way in which your book is marketed will be decided by your publisher, who may or may not consult you and who will claim that market research and experience tells them they are right. Publishers don't have a crystal ball, but it is in their interest to do all they can to make sure your book will sell.

Your job is to pitch the story at the right level of interest for your reader, and to write something that the child in question will not want to put down, no matter what age or gender they are. Look in bookshops and see which publishers publish the kind of books you think you would like to write, and contact them to ask if they have guidelines they can send you. These will usually tell you exactly what will fit in with what they are publishing for that age group, or that imprint. (The imprint is the publisher's way of sectioning their publications into different 'brands' so that the type of book is clear and more recognisable for everyone, from the child to the bookseller. Each imprint has a different style and length, and may or may not include illustrations.) The guidelines may also include information about age and interest level – which will not necessarily be the same; the age level is a guide to the reading age of the child, while the interest level corresponds to the age of a child likely to be interested by the storyline. As no two children are exactly the same, these are always approximate.

Here are some of the categories used by publishers and booksellers, and the kind of books that fit into each.

5–7 years
Books such as *The Queen's Birthday Hat* by Margaret Ryan
This is a lovely example of a book for children who are just beginning to read for themselves. The lively text full of humour and variety and the light, comical illustrations are a perfect fit. We start to feel a little sorry for Queen Forgetmenot on her birthday, because no one seems to be listening to what kind of hat she wants as a gift. And where are the sausages she wants for her breakfast? A lovely, short, page-turning story exactly right for this age range.

Rose Impy's *Titch Witch* series is another good example of this level for newly emergent readers. It features non-threatening text that is well spaced, fun to read and interspersed with cartoon-style illustrations.

Books for the younger end of this age range are usually fairly short, often humorous, and most have illustrations on almost every page – sometimes black and white but often in colour. They are the transition from picture books and tend to look like a novel in size or shape but with much fewer pages. The text is often widely spaced, to make it look less threatening to a new reader.

The text is generally fairly simple vocabulary of the read-it-yourself style for those with newly acquired reading skills. The stories tend to be set in familiar situations, with lots of repetition and patterned language, especially at the lower end of the age range.

For authors writing for 5–7 years, the trick is to make sure that the story is engaging and that any repetition works *for* the story instead of detracting from it. Traditional tales and rhymes work well in this context and humour is always good.

With emerging readers it's important to make sure that they are held by the story, keen to find out what is going to happen next and able to identify with the main character. The stories should enage the reader immediately, because if a child is struggling at all with reading the text, they need to become sufficiently engrossed by the story for it to carry them through. Don't forget that some of the more complicated ideas can be helped along by illustrations, giving you more leeway in the storyline for the less confident reader.

If you are keen to write for this age group, there is no substitute for doing your research. See how other authors have managed to tell a story with short and simple text; examine the books to discover how the illustrations help the story and how dialogue can create a sense of who the characters are and their personalities. Look at where the story begins and how the author has managed to avoid long-winded scene-setting and get straight into the story. Look at what makes you want to turn the page.

For this level it's still a good idea to read your story out loud before you decide that it's finished. It's a good way to see if you have kept the flow of the story.

7–9 (or 6–9) years
Books such as *The Ghost in Annie's Room* by Philippa Pearce

For the slightly older child, books tend to have more text and less illustration, and any pictures they have are usually in black and white. *The Ghost in Annie's Room* by Philippa Pearce is a good example of this; we care about the main character and can feel scared with her. Annie is staying in a strange bedroom in her aunt's house, and she thinks the room is haunted. Running to a length of around 65 pages, the book doesn't look too daunting for the less adventurous reader but the story appeals and is able to hold their interest.

At this age there are often great differences in the reading ability of children; therefore books for the 7–9 age range can vary from simpler short novels to huge doorstop-sized novels which some of the more competent readers in this age range can manage.

Other books for this age level include: *The Tiara Club* by Vivian French; *Horrid Henry* by Francesca Simon; *Clarice Bean* by Lauren Child; and *The Worst Witch* by Jill Murphy. All are based around one or more characters and vary in length. There are also individual 'stand alone' books such as *The Runner* by Keith Gray and *Name Games* by Teresa Breslin. The length of any book should depend on the story, and publishers are leaning towards books being more 'author-led' in this respect.

The story possibilities are almost endless; the more original and engaging, the better. Subject matter might include fairies, football, families, fantasy, real life, humour – as long as it's a good story, well told, it will appeal to this age range.

Make sure that your story, although page-turning and engaging, is not overly complicated and squeezed into shape to fit the level. Avoid too much in the way of detailed description if it is a shorter story; keep it moving with plenty of dialogue and action and not too many characters. You may find it easier if there are only one or two main characters, restricting any others to 'walk-on' parts.

Always keep the reader in mind and ask yourself if they know the main character(s) well enough to care what happens to them. Is there enough happening to keep the reader engrossed? Is the resolution of the story satisfying? Some children can cope with much longer text while others are still put off at this stage by anything too long. This is an age at which short series books (*see* Chapter 4) come into their own.

Children love to collect things, and this also applies to series of books where they get to know the characters and want to collect the entire set. Boys and girls are sometimes drawn to different genres, but they all love humour and believable characters with exciting plots.

With careful use of dialogue and clever use of twists in your story, you can create strong characters and situations that make the reader desperate to see what happens next – despite not having a particularly large word count to play with. Books for this age can vary from between 1500 to 8–10,000 words; again, check the publisher's guidelines to see what they are looking for. There is no point writing a perfectly good story of 1000–2000 words and sending it to a publisher that is only looking for stories of 4000+ words. They will not accept it, and it will only show that you have not taken the time to find out what they are looking for.

If your story is turning out to be too lengthy, you can always cut it back a bit to fit; indeed, sometimes this makes it better. However, be wary of cutting a story too much: it may end too quickly or simply not 'hang together'. In such a situation, you can always look for a different publisher or series.

Writing for this age range can be tricky because there is a wide variation in reading ability and interest. A good strong story that is exciting will always be interesting, but it's a good idea to look and see what has been published for this age range. Different imprints will have their own particular style: some are much slimmer books with short stories that can be read quickly, while others are novel-length books with more complex plots and in-depth characters.

8–12 years (or 8–10 and 9–12)
Books such as Rebecca Lisle's *The Curse of Toads*
Reading skills and text comprehension are well developed at this stage, so you can be more subtle. Some children may still have reading difficulties, but also want to read good stories for their own age group; these readers require slightly different length and format (for more on this, *see* Reluctant Readers, pp. 40–43).

Generally by this stage children can read novel-length books of around 70,000 words, with quite complex storylines and themes running through them – and there has been a recent trend among publishers to produce even longer novels. However, the length of a book is less significant in terms of age level than the way in which the subject matter is treated. A relatively long book may have a light and easy-to-follow plot, while a much shorter book may be more challenging in terms of content. The longer children's book is likely to feature more sub-plots and a bigger cast of characters, because in a shorter book these would be unwieldy.

Having said this, neither plot nor sub-plot(s) should be overly complicated and should all be resolved in one way or another by the end of the book. If the title is to be part of a series or have a sequel, some sub-plots might not be completely resolved, leaving the reader some continuity when they read the next book. This doesn't mean that you can leave the main plot hanging; the sequel may never be published at all for a variety of reasons, and your reader will want some kind of closure for the main characters.

Basically, a story is as long as it needs to be – and this depends upon your judgement and the judgement of your editor. The writer's task is to tailor their story to the right age group, engaging the reader throughout with plot and characterisation without being self-indulgent. Not every child wants to read a book that would make a good doorstop!

Be aware, too, of pace. This should vary during the book but never become so slow that the reader is reluctant to read on. The child reading your book needs to want to find out what is going to happen to the characters, so it is also important that these should be believable and have depth: cardboard cut-outs won't work. The climax of your story should be dramatic or exciting and the resolution satisfying, so as to make the child's experience of reading the book worth the effort. For more information on plot and characterisation, see Section 2 of this book, *A Writer's Toolkit*.

Rebecca Lisle's *The Curse of Toads* is a good example of a novel that is ideal for the average reader in the middle of this age range. Set in 1682 it tells the story of Reuben, whose grandmother and only living relative is hanged as a witch – making him also suspect. He runs away, but are the strange Dr Flyte and his assistant Baggs, who offer him a ride on their cart, really as helpful as they seem? The story carries the reader along with Reuben on his journey marked by intriguing twists and scary turns, as he manages to work his way out of difficult situations in very credible and interesting ways.

Catherine MacPhail writes exciting and realistic contemporary adventure books for this age range, such as *Wheels and Dark Waters*. *Troll Fell* by Katherine Langrish and *Holes* by Louis Sacher are also good reads for this age level.

Books by Anthony Horowitz, particularly the Alex Rider series, and by Jacqueline Wilson have a huge following. For those readers at the top of the age range who like long, involved fantasy stories there are of course the Harry Potter books.

For the teenage reader there is a wealth of books available in all genres. *STRAVAGANZA City of Masks* by Mary Hoffman is the first of a trilogy that has now become a much longer series. This book introduces us to a city that is an alternative Venice. The Philip Pullman trilogy *His Dark Materials* is also for the older reader. Once you venture into the teenage/young adult market books can vary in subject matter from something easy and interesting to read to subjects that are much more difficult in terms of the reader's maturity – which is why this area of writing is best dealt with in more depth than is possible here.

Summing up

Never underestimate your young readers; challenge them and make the characters so real that they want to stay with them long after they have finished reading. Make the climax so exciting that readers wish they could shut their eyes but dare not because they have to stay with the characters. Never create an ending that is so unrealistic that the reader feels cheated; children learn from books, and are able to take on board the reality that everything doesn't always turn out perfectly in life.

If you want to write about real life, remember that your readers are young and impressionable and you should still offer some hope for the future. Make your story a mystery so that readers cannot guess how it will all end, but are delighted when they get there – even if it's sometimes a little sad.

4.

Writing a Series

Sequels, trilogies and series

When you write more than one book about a particular character or group of characters, or perhaps more than one book based in a certain place or world, this might be termed a *series*. One book following on from another can be termed a *sequel*, and three books, a *trilogy*. Definitions can be loose, and categories can cross over.

A series is usually understood to comprise several books – more than two or three. It may be based on the same main character or cast of characters throughout, and perhaps find them consistently in the same location or world (Hogwarts is an example). The titles in a series may or may not have to be read in a specific order.

> *STRAVAGANZA* began as a trilogy but I've now written book four; book five will follow. Bloomsbury has stopped calling it a 'series' and now say it's a 'sequence' – delightfully open-ended.
>
> **Mary Hoffman**

Why write a series?

Children love collecting, and a series of books works well for everyone – child, writer and publisher. There are lots of different types of series books, from short picture books for the very young to novel-length titles for older children. Children enjoy getting to know and like – or dislike! – the characters, and become familiar with the setting.

A series character has to have mileage. You have to like the character – you might, with any luck, be stuck with him or her for a long time. You have to be able to put that character into any situation and know them so well you know what they would do, or say. That character has to drive your story forward.

Catherine MacPhail

A successful series creates both anticipation and security: ultimately both children and parents know what to expect. For younger children, books such as *Horrid Henry* by Francesca Simon work well because readers can see much of themselves in the characters and recognise many of the situations. Children especially enjoy stories featuring exaggerated personalities that are set in normal, everyday situations. Henry is naughty, but very appealing when set against his prissy, perfect brother. He says things that children might often think but don't dare say, and the resultant humour is liberating. Vivian French's *Draglins* is a highly illustrated series for younger children, while longer novels such as the Alex Rider series by Anthony Horowitz have particular 'boy appeal' for an older age group.

Fantasy and series

There is a lot of fantasy written for children and this is a genre that has always leaned towards series. Having created a complex and credible world for your characters, it is comfortable for both writer and reader to step back into it in a second and subsequent tale.

No matter how fantastic the setting or the characters, a fantasy has to have credibility across the whole series. You need to consider what the rules are for your magical world, so that your characters have certain constraints to work within. This can be useful in creating conflict and problems for your characters to resolve. It doesn't work simply to have a character wave a magic wand to solve all their problems, because this removes any challenges and will ultimately irritate or bore your reader. Why would they – or your characters – bother about any problem if there were an instant and simple wand-waving solution to it?

You also need to think about the consequences of using any magical or fantastic abilities. This is all part of the initial construction of your fantasy world: parameters must be set, even if they are not all immediately apparent, and they must be consistent. If you are going to give a character the ability to fly, the reader should be informed of this early in the story, not just before they use it – and it should be followed through across all the series titles. How do they use the ability to fly; do they lose it at some point, and why? What are the consequences?

Your fantasy world needs to have all the elements your characters require to live within it, and how much detail you go into will depend on the kind of story you are writing. But even shorter fantasy books in a series will need quite a lot of thought about the world the characters live in before you start to write anything, so you have a good working knowledge of it. Often much of this will not appear in the book, but it will inform your writing and make the world more credible for your readers.

> You can't cut corners when world-building. Not everyone spends as many years as Tolkien creating a secondary world, but you do really need to know it inside out, so that you could answer a round of *Mastermind* on the details.
>
> **Mary Hoffman**

Series and multiple authors

Sometimes a series is written by a single author, but there are also series where the books appear to have a single author but are actually written by different people using a pseudonym – such as those originated by Working Partners. For their books, the basic idea may come from a publisher or from their creative team. The company then commissions authors to write within the very detailed world and characters already mapped out. Titles are written by different authors but are often sold under a fictitious name, such as Daisy Meadows or Lucy Daniels. Examples include the Animal Ark stories, and for girls – all pink and sparkly – the Rainbow Fairies. The slightly longer Beast Quest series is designed with boys in mind, although girls enjoy the books too. Working Partners series have a wide range of genre and style; although most of their writers will have been found through literary agencies, they will consider unpublished writers.

Although this can be a good way to get published, you have to be able to write within very strict boundaries – which is by no means an easy task. If the company feels that your writing style might suit one of their series, they will send you a kind of 'bible' to follow. This tells you about all the characters, their background and familial relationships and anything else you need to know about the world they inhabit, so that you can write a story to fit. The contact page for writers is on Working Partners' website: www.workingpartnersltd.co.uk.

The company pays the writer an advance against a percentage of the royalty they receive from the publishers, which means that you will get a much smaller advance and royalty than you would if you were writing directly for a publisher. The benefit to you as a writer is that you are likely to have a much bigger volume of sales and substantial marketing to back up the books.

This kind of work is not an easy route into getting published, if such a thing even exists. You have to be able to write well, and not everyone can write within someone else's restrictive boundaries. It may not be for you – but some writers have found significant success this way. They often write other books at the same time.

More generally, if you want to write for an existing series you should do your homework thoroughly. Read books in the series; get to know how the characters – the world they live in, their personalities, how they interact; and think about how the stories were conceived and written. When you eventually approach the publisher, you can then show that you are serious and have taken the time to find out all you can about their books.

Once you have become published in this way, there is nothing to stop you trying to get your own stories published elsewhere or continuing to write for this kind of series as well as writing other material. Either way it can be a good experience.

Creating your own series

To create your own series your stories need to have strong characters and situations that will stand revisiting. Depending on the kind of series you plan to write it's a good idea, before you start, to think about whether the storyline and the situation will have possibilities for several books. The books will still need to stand alone, each a finished story in itself.

> Characters that the reader really cares about are essential for any successful story, but in a good series they must continually grow and develop. If you make the characters real enough you will end the series with fans begging for more.
>
> **Cindy Jeffries**

Be careful that you don't 'write your characters into a corner' by making something final happen or solving an ongoing problem, leaving nowhere to go in the next book. You may start off writing what you think is a single book, but the publisher may see the opportunity to expand on its success and ask you to write a sequel – and then more. Equally, something that starts with the potential of being a series may just not work well enough and you could end up with just one book. This is one good reason why it's important for each story to stand on its own, even within a series.

If you are writing for much younger children there will be fewer lines on each page and there should be lots of repetition. Keep it simple. There might be only four books in a series, but there will be illustrations taking up a lot of the page and carrying some of the story. For the younger reader particularly, the story has to be fun and exciting.

Children like numbers on the spine so that the books are collectable; publishers like this too! Some very commercial series run to 30–40 books or more; the books are usually quite short and, if successful, may be translated into many different languages and have huge print runs. You would then be expected to write a lot – perhaps six books at a time – in quite a short space of time, possibly with added books coming at seasonal periods like summer and Christmas. Hard work, but the rewards for something this successful make it all well worth the effort.

If you have an idea for a series of your own and decide to approach a publisher, there are a few things to bear in mind. Publishers will want to market your idea as a concept, so the design may in part be taken over by their marketing and publicity people – which means you may have to agree to some things you are not too happy about. Bear in mind that these are highly commercial ventures and the publishers, once hooked, will be prepared to throw a lot of money at them. However, they will expect returns and so consequently will be looking at the idea in its entirety and with a very commercial eye.

You may have to be prepared to compromise, but that doesn't mean you cannot suggest things or say when you think something is not right – just be prepared to be outvoted some of the time. If this is not to your taste then you have to decide that very early on and write something entirely different, or approach a different publisher. This is not necessarily something that happens only with a series, and a publisher may suggest a substantial rewrite on a single (someimes called a 'stand-alone') book.

Most series follow a fairly familiar pattern: you have your characters; you set up a problem or some conflict between them; and then you provide a solution. There is usually a story arc that reaches beyond any one book – a continuing theme. This may be the perennial struggle of good against evil, which manifests in an ultimate goal that both sets of characters ('good' and 'bad') are either working towards or trying to prevent. It might be the end of the world as the characters know it, danger to their loved ones, or some other major change in their lives. The complexity of the plot will to a large extent be dictated by the target age group, and by the length of the book. Titles within a series are usually fairly consistent in word count.

Writing any series is hard work. If you are lucky enough to get your own, the publisher will expect you to work to a tight timeframe so that they can keep producing books, and thus keep your readers interested. You have to keep up – not a bad problem for a writer, it's true, but do ensure that you are able to meet any agreed deadlines. Be realistic about what you can achieve within a given timeframe; don't be overly optimistic.

If this happens to you, there may come a time when you decide that you have had enough but the publishers are still keen to continue with the series. This is the point at which you might wish to secure an agreement that allows someone else to take over. In such an event the publishers will commission other writers to continue with the series.

Where to start

Always start with your characters. Who are they, how many? Two is probably too few and more than six is possibly too many – but as always, there are no hard and fast rules. Try to make your characters very different from each other. To get some ideas, look at children around you; think about kids you remember from school; talk to the children of friends and family members. Make sure your characters reflect their different natures. If at all possible, each child who reads your books should feel a connection to one of the characters, feeling that that character is just like them.

Here are some things to consider:

- Gender
- Age
- Race
- Family
- Self-confidence
- Academic ability
- Manual skills

You might want to feature one or more of the following:

- The 'geek'
- The popular child
- The strong personality
- The girly girl
- The tomboy
- The shy one
- The daring extrovert

With age, it's usually good to try and keep the characters within a year or two of each other – or else you need to find a reason why they would be much younger, for example a younger sibling or relative or a step-brother or sister who always has to tag along (and perhaps always gets into trouble).

Think about the conflicts and/or developments that could be caused by pairing or grouping your characters, so that in any situation this might give rise to interaction between them. It may even suggest storylines or sub-plots. The daring extrovert might upset the shy child or irritate the geek; the younger sibling might steal the older child's thunder by coming up with a solution to a problem that he or she wished they had thought of first. Once you know your characters' personalities well, all kinds of possibilities suggest themselves.

Look too at the world your characters are living in; it might be realistic or imaginary, but it needs to have room to expand with the series. Children love stories set in familiar settings but with a twist, or perhaps a magical setting with supernatural opportunities or set in an unusual place.

Watch out for problems that might occur if your series is sold into the big markets such as Australia or the USA. Bunnies are considered vermin in Australia, so a story which features them as characters, or good characters at least, might not go down well there. Issues associated with being 'politically correct' are discussed in more detail on pp. 3–4. If in doubt, seek advice from a publisher or agent – or your editor might pick up on potential problems and recommend some small changes.

As with all children's writing, read all you can. There's no point in creating a great idea for a series that has already been done, or something so similar that no publisher is going to be interested.

How to put your ideas to a publisher

Follow the basic rules set out in Section 3 of this book, under *How to Prepare Your Manuscript*. Here too are some specifics that might help you when presenting a proposal for a series.

Your proposal should consist of:

- Characters and their descriptions in detail – i.e. what makes them different from each other, what keeps them together, what motivates them. If pertinent, include details about the place they inhabit and how that will work in relation to the characters.
- A synopsis for the first 4–6 books, to show where the series is headed and how it will evolve.
- A title. This is important. It may well change, but don't let that prevent you from suggesting a snappy one.
- Characteristics – what is it about the characters that will connect with your readers? Being shy; being bullied; being extrovert?

It is a good idea to send in the first book already completed, unless you are an established writer for this age group. Mention any record of publication you might have and your contact details, in a short introductory letter.

> I have a particular soft spot for series writing because of the joy with which I used to open the latest instalment of something involving familiar characters.
>
> **Helen Salter**

5.

Writing Non-Fiction

I hate describing anything by what it is not. We don't tell a boy he is a 'non-girl', so why do we say 'non-fiction'? It is so much more.

Stewart Ross

Despite its somewhat restrictive name, non-fiction is an incredibly wide and varied field. Simple board books about animals; detailed information about the human body, machines or trees; books about history or our ancestors; facts about the world around us or the skies above – the genre encompasses all of this, and more.

When approaching a publisher for non-fiction, let them know about any experience or expertise you may have in the area you are interested in writing for, and if you have had anything published that is relevant. Enthusiasm for your subject is also appreciated – but particularly if it's backed up by experience.

Most educational publishers commission non-fiction, and there are also several trade publishers that specialise in this area – for example, Dorling Kindersley, Usborne and Watts Wayland. You can find more companies in the relevant section of A & C Black's *Children's Writers' & Artist's Yearbook*.

If you do possess a particular knowledge of some specific subject area, you will be able to write non-fiction with great authority, although much of what is written – particularly for the youngest children – can be researched. If you have an idea for a non-fiction book, it's helpful to have some notion of where it might fit into the school curriculum. This is not because it would have to be sold to an educational publisher; even a trade publisher will want to know that schools will be interested in your book to increase the sales potential. You also have to temper your material to the age range you are writing for.

People think that it's about being an expert, but the most important thing is to write brilliantly.

Nicola Morgan

Even experts don't always have all the answers! Children often imagine that adults know everything, but while non-fiction books need to speak with some authority about their subject matter, it is sometimes good to reinforce the point that children can have ideas, too – and that their views can be equally as valid as those of the experts, who may only have conjecture, not evidence, to base their assumptions on.

Research for ficion can throw up the same kind of problem. Once, I tried to discover whether a pterodactyl would have nested in a tree or on a cliff edge. I needed the information for a book I was writing: *Fizzkid the Inventor*. The expert I contacted told me that no one is completely sure, because there is no hard evidence either way; it would probably have depended on how big the creature was, as pterodactyls came in all sizes. In such a case, the expert uses their background knowledge of the subject to make an assumption. In the end I decided to make my pterodactyl nest in a large tree. This worked better for the story; my fictional character was able to climb the tree to retrieve her time-travelling pogo stick – she had accidentally left it in the nest.

Always try to leave the children something to discover.

Vivian French

When writing non-fiction, you need to think first about how you want to approach your subject. There are always several ways to look at things; one person's worm can be another's dragon. And speaking of worms … Some subjects will draw children in because of the 'yuck' factor. Don't be afraid to take advantage of anything that will engage your reader. Something that they will be fascinated in because it's scary or horrible looking, when presented in a large visual context, will make younger children react and often make them eager to keep on reading.

Decide how you are going to 'hook' your reader. Some non-fiction is presented in a fictional style, which tells a story around the facts. There are quite a few examples of this kind of book, and they tend to be very successful. One such series is Random House's 'Flying Foxes'. Each title has 48 pages and colourful cartoon-style illustrations. In *The Magic Backpack* by Julia Jarman, Josh has forgotten to bring in the cocoa on the day his class are making a chocolate cake – so he takes off with his magic backpack to his uncle's cocoa plantation in Ghana. The book features maps and information about where all the ingredients come from and how cocoa beans are made into chocolate. At the end there is even a recipe in easy-to-follow stages. It reads like a good story but is packed with information.

It is important to make sure that all the known facts about the subject are well researched and well presented, but children often remember the story first and only subsequently, the facts that are embedded within it. Bear in mind that the story has to stand up on its own, not just as a vehicle for the facts. A good story, well told, is essential.

How do you start?

With non-fiction you want to think about the age level you are targeting, how the subject matter will fall in with the curriculum and/or the house style of the particular publisher, and also about layout, illustrations and/or diagrams. These all add to the costs, so if you are being commissioned, the publisher will either have already come up with some layout and design ideas or will want to have some idea of what you have in mind so that they can cost that into the overall budget for the book.

When writing for the school library market, non-fiction may start with the publisher commissioning the author. Alternatively they may approach a packager with an idea or a complete concept, often for a series of books. The packager will get a team together, which will include the author, designer, indexer, researchers and others.

When writing to a commission you might ask for, or be given, a book plan. This will include an outline of how many pages are in the book and how many 'spreads' (a double page, when the book is open flat in front of you, is called a spread). It will also cover:

- Style
  i. If it is to be modern or traditional in style.
  ii. Some publishers have a 'house style' – a particular look to their books that can even include something as specific as their preferred use of commas. Some may even provide style sheets.
- Sample – a visual example of the style and the look/feel.
- Sample text – to show the level required.
- Word count – how many words per spread.

There will be meetings to discuss any ideas the writer may have about layout, and the writer will be asked to present a few sample spreads. If a packager is involved, this will also be sent on to the publisher who will sometimes try to test the market, looking for co-editions to make sure that the books will sell beyond the home market. Creating a non-fiction book can be expensive, so the publishers need to be sure the project is commercially viable.

The illustrator chosen will depend on the publisher or packager, and also on the budget. Sometimes the process will involve sourcing photographs, if these can be acquired and be cost-effective; the writer will be expected to write captions, and also to provide a glossary and any further reference information that is to be included in the book. Sometimes they might be asked to write captions in boxes, but this will be decided at the layout stage.

The writer is usually consulted on the accuracy of the illustrations or photographs. Interestingly, the focus changes with different types of publishers; some will be primarily interested in big glossy images and illustrations, while others will be led by the words. This is principally dictated by the house style.

You have to be aware that there are few prizes, no publicity budget. You need a really marketable subject and, in the current climate, any tie-in with the school curriculum could help.

Jenny Alexander

Writers are usually paid a fee for non-fiction, rather than a royalty (*see* pp. 158–160 for more information). It can be regular work once you get your name known with the publishers or packagers. As packagers tend to be working for publishers, if you want to get into this area of writing you should contact the publisher rather than a packager in the first instance. After working with them, the packagers may then contact you for further work they have been commissioned to do – possibly for a different publisher.

One of the most common complaints about writers seems to be that when they deliver late it upsets everyone's schedule and in some cases can cost the publisher or packager a considerable amount. Be professional, and try to deliver on time. If despite your best efforts it looks like this is going to be a problem (and it can happen to anyone from time to time), contact your publisher ahead of time – not just the day before. This is an issue with packagers especially, where their profit margins and timescales are very tight.

In non-fiction, as with any area of writing for children, there is no excuse for unprofessional behaviour. Writing a book is a lot about being part of a team. It may be true that without the writers there would be no book, but if you want to be treated with respect it is only reasonable to consider the other people working on the same project. When a book is delivered late it can mean other freelancers having their complete work schedule rearranged, and if printing costs are to be kept down publishers need to keep to their projected dates. This is particularly true when working with smaller publishing companies or packagers who may need to have more than one book being printed at the same time, to minimise costs.

6.

Writing for Reluctant Readers

What is a reluctant reader?

There are various terms used when talking about children who find reading difficult or who are unable to read at the levels that are generally recognised to be the accepted norm for their age.

Children vary so much in their development and their tastes that it makes any classification difficult. It can also cause a lot of heartache for both the children and their parents. I firmly believe that children who struggle academically can and do rise above the expectations we may have of them. This is not to say that we should set the bar too high and make them feel inadequate if they don't reach it; rather, we should be aware that as adults we can unwittingly crush a child's confidence, creating in them a sense of failure that can become a self-fulfilling prophecy.

There are definitely children who learn to read at a slower pace than their peers and others who have very real learning difficulties. There are also those who have never found anything in the written word that has excited their interest sufficiently to get them over a disinterest in books and reading. I know of at least one award-winning writer who had this kind of experience, and one book that made the difference – turning disinterest to enthrallment.

The writer's task is to create the most exciting and interesting books they can; books that will grab a child's curiosity at the beginning and make them desperate to read on. This is so much more relevant when the child is a reluctant or struggling reader or has particular problems in that area. The first sentence or

40

paragraph can be the deciding factor as to whether the child will read on or not.

These books need to be immediate, with a plot that is easy to get into and has plenty going on. The story is not convoluted, but also avoids patronising the reader or insulting their intelligence. That doesn't mean it has to be simple – just more accessible. The recognised reading age of the child may have no bearing on their physical age or intelligence and that is where this area of writing becomes fascinating.

> Reluctant readers: They may be reluctant but they're not stupid. Try and make up for complexity of language, etc. by having a very exciting story. If you tell the story in the first person you can make things simpler. **Adele Geras**

You may be asked to write a story that has an interest level to appeal to an older child of perhaps 10+ who only reads at the level of a 6 or 8 year old. This means that the theme of the story has to be sufficiently complex and interesting to keep the child engrossed, with real relevance to their age, interests or problems. At the same time the sentence structure needs to be less complex than would normally be used for that age group, and the vocabulary clear and accessible.

The books also need to be shorter. If you put yourself in the place of someone who finds a task like reading quite difficult, they are likely to be put off by what seems to them to be a huge task – i.e. reading a book of several hundred pages. Lots of action, short paragraphs, and dialogue to break up the text are all key to success.

Most books for reluctant readers are published by educational publishers, who commission them to very strict guidelines. (More information about these guidelines are included in Chapter 7 of this book, on educational publishing.) Writing for children with special educational needs is slightly more complex, and such books are usually commissioned by the publisher – again, generally by educational publishers. Specific briefs let the writer know exactly what is expected of them, but similar rules apply: make it short, exciting, and page-turning.

Barrington Stoke (www.barringtonstoke.co.uk), award-winning trade publishers for reluctant readers, have a unique approach, which has won them many accolades and particular success. They publish books for children and adults who struggle with mainstream books. They have targeted readers from 8 years old to adults, who have reading ages of anything from 6 years upwards.

Authors who write for Barrington Stoke are invited to do so, and no unsolicited submissions from new writers are accepted. As you can see from their website, they commission books only from established writers, because they believe that all children deserve to read books by top writers, whatever their reading ability, and to have access to books which look the same as those their peers are reading.

Their approach is notable in that commissioned authors are not asked to write specifically for reluctant readers; that aspect is dealt with at the editorial stage, to avoid writers altering their style and voice to meet the requirements of the reluctant reader. If the writer is concentrating so hard on making sure the text is simple, the book can get a strained and staccato feel about it rather than flowing well – something that any writer for reluctant or struggling readers has to be wary of.

When the books are written, the manuscript is carefully edited in a consultation process between the language editor and the writer. The final stage is when the manuscript is sent out to children who have agreed to be consultants; they go over the manuscript, noting the parts or specific words that they don't understand or have difficulty reading. Sometimes writers may have ways of expressing themselves that are completely misinterpreted by a reluctant reader, who might take everyday phrases quite literally.

One comment made about a story illustrates this very well. The author had written what seems like a perfectly normal phrase: 'He pushed his glasses up his nose.' The reader's comment was, 'Yuck!'

At this point the language experts and editors work with the writer to fix all the problems that the children have highlighted.

Writing for children who are struggling to read and enjoy books can be very rewarding for everyone concerned. Knowing that you have created something that may help a child discover the joys of reading is especially gratifying – even more so if it has been the first book that child has ever managed to read.

When a reader is hooked on a story, his or her reading ability is proven to improve. They read more fluently – because they want to read on!   **Barrington Stoke**

7.

Writing for the Primary School Educational Market

Definition – Educational publishers Publishers of schoolbooks: fiction and non-fiction written almost exclusively for use in schools.

> I'll never forget the first book I learnt to read at school: *Little Red Hen*. It was part of a reading scheme and I can still remember every word. There were only 12 of them, but having mastered them one by one, I knew I'd cracked the magic code.
> **Jeanne Willis** (Harcourt Reading Information Leaflet 2007)

Writing for the educational market has many positive aspects, and just one of these is the impact you can make if your book is one of the first in a child's life. The work is often demanding, but it can be highly rewarding.

Let me first dispel one myth: you don't have to be a teacher to write educational books successfully – although many children's writers are or have been teachers. Never having been a teacher myself, I come at it from a writer's point of view and I think that gives me a different perspective.

In this market you may come across a lot of 'jargon' – phrases, words and acronyms frequently used by teachers and others involved in the teaching profession. This can be confusing, but in fact the terms are not complicated and will be explained if you ask for clarification. However, it is good to get to know some of the basics. In England, Northern Ireland and Wales there is the National Curriculum with Key Stages 1–4. The Key Stages relate to four different age brackets – for example, Key Stage 1 relates to children aged under seven years who are in Years 1 and 2 in schools. In Scotland the new 'Curriculum for Excellence' is gradually being rolled out; this takes over from the 5–14 guidelines and becomes applicable to children aged 3–18 years. This and other information is available on websites of the relevant education authorities: you may consult these if there is something particular that you really need to know.

If you do happen to be a teacher, the chances are that you actually understand and possibly even speak this rare and peculiar language. But for the rest of us, it is possible to survive and indeed thrive in this market by just learning the bare essentials.

Educational versus trade publishing

Most of what we have looked at so far has been trade publishing. Trade publishers are those who publish the books you are likely to find in bookshops and libraries: fiction, non-fiction, picture books and everything in between. Trade titles also include home learning books that parents might buy themselves, if they are teaching children at home or wish to add to their child's educational experience in school. Home learning books are usually, but not always, published by trade publishers, so that they are available to parents rather than teachers. Some home learning books are published by educational publishers and then sold into bookshops on what they call 'trade terms'; this means at a higher discount on the selling price than they would grant for their school books.

Educational publishers

These publishers publish books specifically for use in schools – books that teachers hand out to schoolchildren in the classroom. So the main difference between trade and educational publishers is that educational publishers sell their books directly into schools, to the teachers. The books are teaching tools and are frequently sold in class packs, 6–8 of each title. This means that the teachers can use them with small groups of children, since they rarely require each child in a class to have the same book at the same time. Titles may be part of extensive reading-book series such as OUP's (Oxford University Press) Oxford Reading Tree, which has been in print for many years. Not all schools will buy in a complete new reading scheme because it is an expensive business, so some will use selected parts of a new scheme to enhance the stock of books they already have, gradually building it up. There are also books dealing with specific subjects such as history, geography, science and so on.

From the point of view of the children's writer, one of the interesting differences is that trade books are published and promoted under the author's name, while educational books tend to be sold and promoted under the publisher's name and the name of the series – unless the author is already well known. Because there may be many different authors writing parts of a large educational series, it is not always practical for the publisher to promote all of the authors involved, so that teachers may recognise the series but not be immediately aware of who wrote the individual books.

This gives rise to the strange comment often seen in educational publishers' catalogues, that the stories are written by *real* authors – although not having met any 'unreal' authors, I am often taken aback by this! One editor rather sheepishly admitted to me recently, 'Well yes, we do promote the series name rather than the authors, but we also want it both ways and we will mention by name well-known trade authors, when we get them to write for us.' As a result, when you are published in this market and look for your book online, you will find that beside it will be the name of the series, the ISBN number and cost, but only a minor indication of who the author is – and at times none at all.

> Some people may suggest that writing for the educational market is not as good/important/clever as writing mainstream. Your books won't appear on bookshop shelves, people won't recognise your name, advances are not high – you can forget the six-figure sum ... [However] your books may stay in print for years, you will keep getting royalties for them, and they may well earn out their advance several times over.
>
> **Lynne Benton** (educational author)

One editor has suggested that the educational market can provide higher returns from bulk series sales than from single-copy sales in the trade market – which is a valid point. If you write for a long-running and successful series it can provide a good income for a number of years.

Ideas for the educational market

In terms of ideas and content, there are lots of possibilities. Perhaps you might like to write fiction; in the educational market this often comprises reading books for children who are learning to read or improving their reading skills, and they can be great fun to write. It can also include longer texts for more established readers: here, teachers are looking to introduce carefully levelled material suitable for particular ability levels, or to widen the field to include different types of stories, such as folk tales and the re-telling of familiar stories. Myths and legends fit in here, too.

There are also stories from different cultures, and those which tackle issues such as bullying or racism, but in a fictional context; this can promote discussion in the classroom or expand on a subject in the curriculum. Bear in mind that in educational publishing, books are almost entirely commissioned by the publisher, so it is unlikely that subject matter will arise directly from an author's suggestion.

It is more likely that the publisher will approach an author with a detailed brief for something they have already decided to publish. You can approach an educational publisher with an idea for a book or series of books on a particular subject, but it would need to fulfil some particular requirement of the curriculum and be something that the publisher thinks would be universally useful to teachers. Even then it may not fit in with their planning at that time.

Alternatively you may be interested in writing non-fiction, poetry or plays for schools; want to use any specialist knowledge you may have to write science or maths books for primary schools; or write workbooks that teachers will use in the classroom. I would suggest that in the case of workbooks you need to have some teaching experience in schools, because – unlike with fiction or non-fiction – these need to be particularly geared towards teachers' specific requirements. Often they are used to expand on themes in the curriculum, and/or to extend the usefulness of specific books read in the classroom.

Illustrators in the educational market are generally paid a fee, rather than royalties, but if you are an illustrator you might think of this as a potential market for your work. But be prepared for very tight timescales. If this market is of interest, you could send in some samples of your illustrations for consideration.

As an author, another difference between trade and educational is that you really get no choice in who will illustrate your books. That is up to the publisher, although you should be asked to check the illustrations for errors at proof stages.

Approaching an educational publisher

When deciding to approach an educational publisher, how do you choose? You might ask your local school what books they use for reading, or for maths or science. Ask if you can have a look at their educational publishers' catalogues; better still, see if you can borrow some of the catalogues over a weekend. Look online at educational publishers' websites (although these can be rather confusing, even if you know the market). The best way to get to know what is currently being published is to familiarise yourself with the different imprints of different publishers. If you are looking on a publisher's website and click on Literacy, you will be shown some of the various imprints within their list. Each of these features different series. If you have children of primary school age, look at who publishes the books they are bringing home – but also have a look at the copyright page, which will tell you the year of publication so that you can find out how recently that series was published.

All this will help you build an overview of who publishes what, and what a particular series is about. Add to your knowledge by consulting A & C Black's *Children's Writers' & Artists'*

Yearbook or MacMillan's *The Writer's Handbook Guide to Writing for Children* to find educational publishers who publish in the primary school sector. You can call and ask to be sent a catalogue; these, whether hard copy or online, will tell you a lot about that particular publisher's list. You will find information about each series, and often a sample page to show both look and style. The blurb will tell you who that series is aimed at.

Your research will reveal that the 'major players' in the primary school market now are Pearson Education, whose imprints include the Longman Book Project, Pelican, and Pearson Interactive (and whose recent acquisition of all the Harcourt brands means that they now own Ginn and Rigby-Heinemann UK, thus condensing the market quite a bit), and Oxford University Press (OUP). However, there are other several other publishers with a smaller market share that are worth considering when you want to make a submission. Things are always changing, so it is often productive to do some research to get to know who is publishing what.

Areas such as poetry, plays and non-fiction are covered in other sections of this book, but these are also sectors of the educational market where editors will be looking for writers who can write to a particular level, research a subject and produce work to a specific brief.

> Working for educational publishers gives you fantastic freedom to try different things because you aren't having to build yourself as a brand as you do for trade. **Jenny Alexander**

I have spoken to a few editors recently to see how they would like to be approached by someone wanting to write for them. One particular thing stood out from the rest: *you must act professionally*. I can't stress this enough. If writing for children is something you are just toying with before you go back to your proper day job, remember that this *is* their job. So if you want them to take you seriously, you have to be professional, too.

This applies equally to trade publishing, but in educational publishing everyone is working to extremely tight schedules to make sure that the books are available in time for changes in the curriculum or when the government makes money available to schools. At times they want to publish before their competitors, so they are often not able to move their publication dates to accommodate late delivery of a typescript.

> Get familiar with the curriculum, get familiar with the publisher's list, then submit to a particular series. It's about experience and perception.
>
> **Brenda Stones** (Freelance educational editor and writer)

Make the first approach by sending in a story rather than a letter/email enquiry on its own. This gives them a chance to see if you can write and gives you less chance of falling at the first hurdle because the editor does not have to respond to you twice (they have very little time to spare).

> Don't just send a letter or email, send a story too – something that can be read quickly, that gives us a feel for your writing.
>
> **Mary Hamley** (Senior Editor – Pearson Education)

Some publishing houses are not keen to receive unsolicited work at all, so if you have checked with their website and it says 'no unsolicited manuscripts', remember that sending your story to them is just asking for a rejection. A quick email enquiry stating your interest and any relevant experience might work better.

> New authors should research the key series of each publisher so that they are submitting within the parameters of a particular series.
>
> **Brenda Stones** (Freelance educational editor and writer)

The story is the main thing. Remember that the editor can help to cut it and make it fit a particular reading level, but what they want first and foremost is someone who can write entertaining and exciting stories.

What should be in your cover letter?

Along with the story you need to send a short letter. As with any other submissions when writing for children, the editor will not be interested if your niece or grandchild has loved the story; telling them that will only signal that you are inexperienced. They will be more impressed with any publishing history you may have, or expertise in any specifically related field – for example, if you are writing non-fiction about mountains and you are or have been a mountaineer.

If none of that applies to you, show that you understand the market. Get to know the different series in the market, and tell the editor where your work might fit in: 'I've looked carefully at your Treetops series, and I think that my story might fit in at around level 10.' This tells them you know the market and have taken time to find out what they publish. It also shows that you can write to a specific level, even if they later commission you to write for a different series or level.

If you are sending in an enquiry and short piece of writing by email, which is used increasingly by editors and agents, do check first. They may express a preference to receive submissions as hard copy, and it will serve you well to do everything you can to comply with their wishes (in this and other respects). There is little point in starting off on the wrong foot if someone does not like to be contacted by email, or vice versa.

Understanding the process

It might be useful at this point to tell you how I started out. The first books I got published were for Ginn's 'Zoom' series, for children with special educational needs – that is, for children aged 8–9 with a reading age of 5–6. I had read somewhere that Ginn might be looking for writers for a special needs series, so I contacted my local school. I was lucky in that the school had just received copies of a new series of books by Ginn and I was able to borrow a few of the titles over a weekend. I looked at the content and style of the stories; I counted how many pages per book and words per page; and I looked at the pictures and at the sentence length.

I then wrote a short story that I felt fitted in with their latest series, complying with the average word count and trying to pitch it correctly at the interest and vocabulary levels I had seen in the books I'd borrowed. I didn't know at the time that the series was completed and they were no longer commissioning for it, but in the end that didn't matter at all. What was important was that it was a strong story and of similar length and ability level. I looked up Ginn in *Writers' & Artists' Yearbook* and called the switchboard to ask the name of the editor I should send my work to. Armed with this information I sent off my submission, mentioning the series that I felt it fitted into. I then waited to get the usual rejection letter.

Happily the editor replied, saying that although this series was completed she had passed my story on to a colleague who was commissioning a new one. Within a couple of days I got a call asking if I would submit ideas for a series of eight books; my ideas were accepted and soon I was a published writer!

Part of this was probably luck, in that at the time I wrote they were just about to commission another new series for which my writing was suitable – but it was still essential to have done the background work before sending anything in. If at the time you write in, the editor is not actively commissioning, any letter you send will most likely be filed away. Unfortunately the reality is that because editors are so busy, your precious correspondence will probably moulder away in a file – even though it might have achieved a positive result had it arrived at a more opportune moment. For this reason gentle persistence is more likely to achieve success than a one-off 'do or die' approach. If the response to your enquiry was 'thanks but not just now', don't be too downhearted; instead make a note in your diary to contact the editor again a few months later, by which time there might be something new happening.

Writing to a brief

In a publisher's brief, a stage or level might be defined slightly differently from company to company, but it will always tie in with the age of the children together with their reading ability and recognised levels within the curriculum. Some publishers give them names; others, numbers (Level 1, Level 2, or Blue Level, etc.).

Reading age and interest level are often quite different. A child's reading age can be higher or lower than their actual age; it is linked to their ability to read and judged against the ability of an 'average' child. The interest level is more akin to the age of the child. Thus you can have a child aged 8 years with an interest level of 8 years (i.e. subject matter that will interest an 8 year old) but with a reading age of only 6 years (their ability to read is similar to that of an average 6 year old).

A publisher's brief for a new educational series consists of the following:

- The general aims of the series. Who it's targeted at, what stage and whatever specific different thing about it the publishers have come up with to fit into the curriculum.
- A detailed table of how many stages or levels in the series. This refers to age/reading or interest level.
- The general layout of how many books per stage. This can vary widely, in terms of the number of pages per book, the number of words per book, and the number of words or sentences per page.
- A vocabulary list.

Jeanne Willis made me laugh when I read her comments about The List:

> You are strictly forbidden to deviate from The List. Your plot may be worthy of the Booker, but if for example you are delinquent enough to feature a giraffe when 'giraffe' isn't on The List, you'll be put in detention and made to rewrite it all over again, using the words 'Rat', 'Cat' and 'Mat' until you have learnt your lesson.
> **Jeanne Willis** (Harcourt Reading Information Leaflet 2007)

I usually try to ignore the list after a first glance, at least until the story is written. Then I go back and edit viciously. Interestingly enough, the latest approach is not to have words cued solely by the pictures – or at least not to have that as the main issue – because phonics (not a new system, but recently revived) is the latest thinking in teaching literacy. When the text is cued by the pictures, the child can be encouraged to guess what a word in the text might be by looking at the pictures. This method is still used, but phonics at the simplest level encourages the child to learn by reading words that have similar spelling/sound patterns. This is not something that will be used in a specific way by the publisher to fit in with the way in which they want to develop their particular reading series: their requirements of the writer will be fully explained by the publisher's brief.

As regards 'taboo' subjects, there are usually fairly good guidelines within any brief. If you are in any doubt as to whether something you want to write is likely to be contentious – and thus rejected – your editor will be quite happy to advise you. Books that are to be given out by teachers as required reading must not be offensive in any way to parents. This is a realm in which political correctness comes into its own with a vengeance.

The countries in which books are to be sold will often dictate how stringent the taboos are. One series that was to be sold in the USA as well as in the UK was limited by severe stipulations from the American editors: no witches, no warlocks, no spells or incantations, no use of the word 'magic', no monsters or dragons, no pirates ... and on it went. I was most amused when one editor, well on in the commissioning process, asked me if I could write some fantasy for the series. I asked her, 'What with? You've just taken away almost all the fantasy ingredients!' In the end they accepted a story featuring some very nasty trolls. Because the trolls were competing with elves, this had a traditional story/folk tale slant and so was permissable. If a series is only for sale in the UK, all this is usually slightly less of a problem.

Layout

When writing a short, illustrated text you are usually told how many pages will be in the book. I find it easiest to lay my template page out as below, up to the number of pages given. This helps ensure that the story is 'paced' across the book so that it doesn't end too quickly, or try to run on with too many pages. It also reminds me to include some kind of illustrative brief, and shows where the double-page spreads will be so I know I can make the story more exciting by creating suspense where the page has to be turned.

Example:

> Page 9 (right-hand page)
> *Illus: two half-page images.*
> 1) *The family followed by Zoola running up a winding stone stair-case casting large monster-like shadows on the walls beside them*
> Everybody ran up the dark and spooky steps.
> 2) *They have arrived at a creepy looking door with a ghostly door-knocker on it. The sound CREAK! as the door is opening to show dark shadows inside.*
> They came to a dark and spooky door.
> The door opened and there was …
> Page 10 (left-hand page)
> *Illus: The family and Zoola startled by the huge ghostlike figure shouting OOOH! as it comes out of the open door.*
> … the ghost!
>
> *Zoola and the Ghost* by Linda Strachan (originally published by Ginn & Company 1996)

The illustrative brief is not meant to be a complete description, rather an indication of what the picture should show, to guide the illustrator and make everything clear to the editor.

Confidentiality

Educational publishers work in an incredibly competitive market with a few 'key players' competing for the largest chunk of the schools' business. This is often led by the news of government funding in one area or another that is going to become available in x number of months/years. News of this kind sets the educational publishers off to design something that teachers will want to spend that money on. Sometimes they get it right – and sometimes they don't!

Because of the fierce competition and the amounts of money involved in devising, commissioning and producing an educational series, publishers are understandably keen to keep their ideas confidential. If you are sent a brief for an educational series you are usually expected to keep it confidential until the series is published. You do need to heed the confidentiality clause, which is often in your contract – especially as it is likely you may want to work for them again.

Trialling

Once you have written your story, the editor seems happy with it, you have seen the roughs, and everyone and their great aunt has commented on and made changes to layout, text, illustrations, etc. your book is ready to go out to some specially selected schools for 'trialling'. This is where it is tested out on teachers and children, and it is also where your precious story can fall at the last hurdle. I have only had this happen to me once, when not only my book but also the entire top level of a series was scrapped because it didn't sit right with the schools.

This can be quite depressing, because although you will have been paid your advance by this time, all you end up with is a copy of the proofs. You usually keep the copyright and the ability to sell the story on, but chances are it will need to be completely revamped if you do try to sell it elsewhere because it will have been written to a very specific set of criteria.

I once wrote four books for the first level of a new series.

These were published, but a further six books I wrote for the second level never came out because the series was scrapped, leaving the four published books sitting out on their own and not doing very well at all. I was well paid, keeping the advance for the work on all ten books, but I had hoped that the royalties for these would begin to take over as some of my earliest books started to go out of print. Of course, that didn't happen. It must also have been miserable for any new writers writing for that series who would have been hoping to see their first books in print.

There is no real way to avoid such situations, and you can only hope that the advance you have been paid recompenses you for the time spent writing. Bear in mind too that you may eventually get the opportunity to sell these stories on in a slightly changed format.

Agents and educational publishing

As an educational writer, one of the problems of being pretty much invisible is that you are unlikely to find an agent unless you get published in the trade as well. One educational editor told me that most authors seem to think trade is more glamorous, and educational publishing the poor relation. I personally think that it's the trade editors who have that opinion and who are often less interested in your publication record if you 'only' have educational books to your name.

Some agents are not keen to take on educational writers who do not also write trade books. This is because they cannot sell any extra rights, and the income can often be minimal and spread over a long period, not making much for the agent and not promoting their author very much either. (For more information on agents, *see* Section 4.)

Contractual matters

As a writer for the educational market you may be paid either royalties or a fee. If you receive royalties and are lucky enough to write for a series that becomes a core reading scheme, this can be a good pension plan: for example, the Oxford Reading Tree books were introduced into schools about 25 years ago and the series is still going strong. If you write for an educational series that ends up as one of the long-running favourites, you will have a very nice royalty income for a good number of years – long after all the work has been done. But of course there are no guarantees: some series last 4–5 years, some longer, and some much less – although even this can be longer than many single-title trade books last.

You may find a clause in your contract about not writing 'competing works'. What your publisher wants to be sure of is that you are not going to write a similar book for a competitor, thus taking away sales. I personally ask for such clauses to be omitted. If you are writing a lot of educational books, the best thing may be to consult the Society of Authors, or your agent if you have one.

More information on contractual matters is included in Section 4 of this book.

Summing up

You are not likely to make your fortune as a children's writer; very few people do. But if you are a successful educational writer, you can sometimes create a regular income stream in an otherwise precarious career – even if it means that your name may not become well known. Your educational titles may stay in print for ten years or more – not necessarily enough to buy the yacht, but earning you royalties on a regular basis. Educational writing also gives you the very real satisfaction of helping children learn to read and discover the joy of a good story well told.

8.

Poetry and Plays

There are not a lot of openings to publish poetry for children. Collections of poetry are usually written by established and familiar names; sometimes they are augmented with traditional rhymes or those that have been handed down for generations – playground rhymes, for example.

> To write a poem intended for children risks being patronising and/or twee or horribly jolly. The market for a collection of poems for children is incredibly difficult for all but the big names. Best to consider trying to get your work published in anthologies.   **Diana Hendry**

New or unknown writers are unlikely get their own collection of poetry for children published, but if you can get one or more of your poems into an anthology they will be seen and read. You then have a chance of being asked to contribute to another anthology – thus getting you onto what John Foster, well-known children's poet, calls the 'poetry roundabout'.

One way to get started would be to submit a handful of poems to someone who is compiling an anthology. Basically the rules here apply as much as in any other area of writing for children. Don't send in more than four or five poems at any one time, or you will just irritate the person compiling the anthology. Pick those that you feel fit in with the theme or style required for that particular publication. Be professional in your approach, and be prepared to have your work rejected or possibly edited. Having submitted more than one poem, there is a better chance of at least one of them being accepted.

Be very wary of vanity publishing (*see* also page 114). You should not be asked to pay to get your poetry published in an anthology; if you are, it can cost you dearly. Many scams exist that prey on people's vulnerability – so be aware. Everyone likes to see their work in print, and some unethical organisations take advantage of this for their own gain. Of course you may decide to self-publish, and that is a different matter: more information on this is given on page 115.

There are some openings for poetry within the educational market, but even here editors may be more inclined to approach a name they know or use poems that have come from elsewhere, rather than commission new poetry. Schools do like poetry that the teachers can target specifically to the curriculum, so if you want to go down this road the key thing is to investigate the curriculum headings about form ('list poems', 'shape poems', 'patterned poems', etc.) and then contact the editor rather than sending in, for example, thematic 'poems about trees' on spec.

What makes it poetry as opposed to prose? Non-rhyming poetry can be a challenge and, as with poetry for very young children, tends to need strong rhythm. Poetry such as syllabic, haiku or rap lends itself well to children counting syllables and seeing how patterns emerge. This can help differentiate between poetry and prose.

> We want to write about the big things in life, but the way in is through the wee everyday things.   **Liz Niven**

Teachers will often use poetry not written specifically for children. An example of this would be an anthology such as 'The Rattle Bag' edited by Ted Hughes and Seamus Heaney, which contains poems that are appreciated by both adults and children. On the other hand, a dedicated children's book is more likely to be bought by schools concerned to steer clear of a book containing even one poem they think parents might complain about.

Plays

Networking is important if you want to write plays for children's theatre. Get to know the people in the industry by attending talks or perhaps a playwriting course. The BBCwritersroom website www.bbc.co.uk/writersroom/ gives lots of useful information for the would-be children's playwright, as well as downloadable script formats for radio, TV and theatre plays.

Always bear in mind that plays for the theatre need to be commercially viable. Therefore you need to keep the number of actors required to as few as possible – perhaps only two or three. Remember too that theatre for children needs to be short and snappy because of their attention span and the amount of time that children will happily sit with their interest engaged.

The main market for plays for children in book form is in the educational sector, where they can be used in the classroom. There have been several educational series dedicated to plays – for example, Ginn, Letts, and Collins Spotlight – but it is not a huge market. One publisher told me that teachers often ask for plays, but when they are published, for some reason they don't seem to be that popular. These things tend to be cyclical, and if you are keen to write plays the answer might be to either persevere, or to wait for the right time without huge expectations.

Sometimes well-known stories are rewritten in play form and simplified for young readers. One of the challenging things about writing plays is that they are almost all dialogue. With only small amounts of stage direction, the entire plot and characterisation has to come through in the words and actions of the characters. This is a good discipline for strong characterisation in your writing. Keep the plot simple, but you might want to try to put in some kind of twist in the end.

Consider writing short plays for small groups for class work; perhaps four or five characters each with just a short sentence or two at a time. Otherwise there are plays that have many characters, and can be used for an entire class. Sometimes each part is marked in a different colour across the text for each character, or denoted by some other visual clue or symbol, which makes it easy for children to know when it is their part.

Children who have difficulty reading often enjoy having a part in a play that has just a line or two to read at any one time. They will often put so much more meaning into the dialogue than they would if it was part of an ordinary story they had to read.

Other areas where plays for children are required are those to be produced in theatre or film, or on TV. There are some excellent screenwriting and playwriting courses and organisations out there, and if this is the avenue you want to pursue, see under *Useful Information* at the back of this book to find out more.

9.

Research

The Internet is a wonderful resource for the children's writer, offering information on almost any subject. It is therefore a good starting point for your research, helping you to gather some initial facts and ideas and pointing the way to further sources. Bear in mind though that not all the information posted on the Internet is reliable – so it's good idea to keep a note of the pages you visit. In this way you can go back to them if you need to verify or clarify what you found out.

Think carefully about what you need to know before you start your research. Once you start searching in a productive place, you are likely to discover lots of other avenues of enquiry you had not previously considered. Libraries are a wonderful place to get help and information, and librarians can be incredibly helpful in finding sources and books you might need. Often it's only when you start to ask people questions that you discover their depth of knowledge; most people are delighted to speak to you if you tell them you are doing research for a book, and they will go out of their way to help. At times the resultant flood of information can be a little overwhelming, but you will learn to filter it and define what is necessary and what is superfluous.

Speaking to people about their personal experiences can be useful, too. I have found that it helps to record reminiscences (with the person's permission, of course) so that I can listen again later and reflect on which parts are important so I do not have to rely on my notes or memory.

Doing research for a teenage novel I visited the local ambulance control centre and was able to go out with an ambulance crew as an observer. I also managed to get permission to watch fire training school on one of their training days, where they staged a fake car crash so that they could extract people from cars that were on their side or upside down. I watched them cut the cars apart. Everything that you experience – the noise, the smell, the sense of urgency – can be used to add credibility to your writing.

Once you have done your research, beware of using it all just because it's so exciting or interesting. A sprinkling of information, or digested research that informs your story or characters, is much more effective than a lump of indigestible information that is included just because you discovered it and thought it was fascinating. Even in non-fiction it's important to know what to put in and what to leave out.

Remember not to let your research show; it should inform what you write but not be obvious to your reader. Consider setting the information aside for a while: coming back to it after a gap can reveal aspects that previously had not seemed relevant or useful.

Research can be fascinating and beguiling, but be careful not to get so engrossed in it that you neglect to start writing! There will always be access to more and more information: make sure you use only what you need.

Section 2
A Writer's Toolkit

10.

Writing Basics

Don't tell me the moon is shining; show me the glint of light on broken glass.   **Anton Chekhov**

There is a basic set of skills you need if you are to progress as a writer, and once you have mastered these you will be able to adapt them to suit your own particular style.

Writing is something that flows and changes. Everyone has their own idea about how it works best for them, which is why many things you read about writing seem to be contradictory. The minute someone says this is the way it is, or should be, you will find someone else whose experience contradicts it. I have found the best policy is to see what works best for you, but also to be prepared to learn all the time. Of course that doesn't mean you have to change the way you write each time the wind blows in a different direction; to find your own preferred way of working and what works for you, you must try things out and be open to new ideas and working methods.

So there are no absolutes – but there *are* some basics that you need to learn before you are experienced enough to consider abandoning them. If you are serious about getting published you have to think of writing as a skill that may need to be honed before it's quite ready for publication.

The only way to write is to actually write the words. That may sound silly, but many people spend so much time thinking about writing that they rarely get anything written at all. This is one reason for the short exercises at the end of each part of this section. They are intended to give you a starting point, but they may even spark off an idea that could lead you to publication.

A story is like a kid – put the right things in, draw the right things out, and anything is possible ...

Joan Lennon

So you have pen, pencil or perhaps computer poised and ready – but where do you start? Let's look at some of the tools you need in your writer's toolkit.

11.

Ideas

The classic question most writers get asked is, 'Where do you get your ideas from?' I can understand how this can seem like a huge problem, but in reality it's less of a problem than you might imagine. It's not so much that successful writers have better ideas; it's how they use what they see and hear around them that counts.

Ideas can come from anywhere and everywhere:

- A child's question or comment. Children look at the world differently from adults; they see everyday things from a fresh perspective. Listen to children speaking – on the bus, in a supermarket, anywhere. When my son was about three he confidently told me that pavements would grow into buildings.
- A traditional tale from a completely different angle. See it through the eyes of a minor character or a new one of your own. Traditional tales are wonderful source material, but you must make them new and fresh.
- The words of a song or a nursery rhyme. A single phrase out of context may conjure up ideas.
- Putting completely different or opposite characters together in a situation to see what happens.

How to generate fresh ideas

If there is one particular area or genre that interests you, try making a mindmap or spider diagram of words or phrases that can develop into ideas (*see* Exercise 1, below).

One of the best ways to make this work is to brainstorm – i.e. write down the first thing that comes into your head. Once you have as many words or phrases as you can think of, you can move to the next stage.

Look at what you have written and see what interests you most. You might want to try two or more phrases/words together and see if they can suggest a storyline. That is just the idea; the rest of the fun comes next, when you take the idea and let it run free to see what kind of story you can make out of it.

Another way I like to generate ideas is to build a couple of characters (*see* pp. 78–83). Often the characters will suggest a story as you create them. Remember that it's the conflict between two different ideas or characters that will create your story; the conflict could be something as simple as a question in the mind of a character and the different ways in which they try to answer it.

Ideas can be generated in many other ways. Some are suggested below, and in other areas discussed in this section (for example, from dialogue or plot). Most important of all is to *keep looking at the world with a fresh eye* and to listen to what people, especially children, say and how they say it. Take a new look at your own childhood and in particular at memories that evoke emotions. Little cameo memories of childhood can immediately re-create the emotion you felt at the time. Ideas are all around you and all you have to do is to stop, look, listen and perhaps remember. Give the ideas space and let them happen.

Exercise 1

This involves creating a spider diagram or mind map. Take a single word and put it in the middle of a blank sheet of paper. Underline it.

From that word, draw a line out and write another word or a phrase – anything that might relate to the word in any way. Keep doing this until you can't think of any more. Some of the words might spark off ideas of their own, so they in turn would get lines from them to other words and so on.

Step away and look back at the words. See what you might want to use from there as a character or a story; it might be a

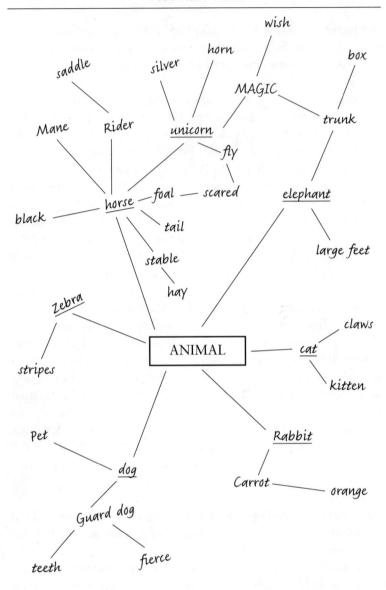

ANIMAL *(and from that might come)* cat, rabbit, dog, horse, zebra and elephant. From horse might come black, mane, tail, unicorn, bay, foal, stable, hay, rider, saddle. From unicorn might come horn, magic, silver, fly, wish, and so on.

story about a zebra and an elephant who come across a horse that really wanted to be a unicorn – or perhaps thinks he is? Try your own mind map and see where it takes you.

Exercise 2
This exercise uses a phrase from a nursery rhyme or song: Take a traditional tale or nursery rhyme, or a line from a song as the centre of your spider diagram and use it to generate ideas. Group one or two words together. You might want to use two of these together or they may just spark off an idea that takes you in a different direction. This exercise is all about freeing up ideas and playing with them, then building on that until you are so excited you can't wait to see where the story takes you next.

Exercise 3
Take an ordinary occurrence, such as opening a school bag, and ask yourself 'What if?' It can be something that might happen in real life, or something completely imaginary.

What if ... you came home from school and opened your school bag to discover that your new mobile phone had turned into an unexploded bomb and your weird new friend seemed to know too much about it. Would you end up on a secret mission to save the world?

What if ... you had been at the museum and some rare artefact was in your bag when you opened it?

Exercise 4
Have a look at picture books that deal with common fears among young children, such as fear of the dark, or starting school, or being left out or forgotten because of a new baby. See how the story has been approached and then see if you can come up with a way to approach that same fear from a new direction.

I write for children because I have vivid memories of childhood and – maybe – because I have never quite grown up!

Griselda Gifford

12.

Plot

A series of exciting incidents does not constitute a plot.

Mary Hoffman

Planning

Ask five different writers, and you will be told five different ways of writing. This is particularly true about planning a story. Some like to have everything planned out to the last detail before they start; others start and after a bit begin to plan where the story will go. Some will have a vague idea of the main points of the plot but are happier letting the story grow organically in between, and others know where the ending is but have no real idea which way the story will go to get there. No way is right or wrong – choose the way that works for you.

Whichever way you write, your story does need to have some kind of structure. There has to be a climax to which the story builds, and at the end all the points of the plot need to be resolved. Think about the story arc – how the plot works throughout the story as a whole, and how it rises to the climax before curving back down to a resolution.

In a longer story there can be several climactic points that leave the reader desperate to know what happens next. The final one should always be the most interesting and exciting, or perhaps the most unexpected, so that the reader comes away feeling satisfied and not let down at the end.

When planning your story you need to think about various aspects, as follows.

Conflict

At the simplest level, this could be created through different answers to a particular question. Alternatively you may have conflict between your characters either because of their personalities, or because of what they want from a given situation. At times the conflict can even be the environment: your characters are confronted with bad weather which stops them from reaching their goal; or perhaps the weather brings out the best or worst traits in the characters, causing conflict between them; or they might have a struggle to survive desperate conditions.

Completeness

A story needs to be complete. The reader wants to feel satisfied that the story has reached a reasonable end, even if it is not exactly what they might have wanted to happen. All your storylines should be resolved by the end. There is no point introducing a storyline that trails off in the middle or one that does nothing to further the story or enhance the reader's understanding of the characters.

Correctness and being 'PC'

Is your story appropriate to children of the intended age? There is no point offering a story about teenage pregnancy to a seven-year-old; it's outside their area of interest.

Creativity

Make sure your story is original. Even a familiar story or idea can be told in an original and interesting way, to move it away from the obvious and make it exciting for the reader.

Capability (understanding)

Think about the target age level for your story. Are your characters slightly older than your reader? Is the way the story is told appropriate to the age of the reader, in simplicity or complexity of plot as well as language?

Starting to plot

Your plot is the skeleton of your story. Without a plot there is no story – but without conflict, however minor, you have no plot.

A story for younger children will have a more linear and straightforward plot. It may have several 'layers', but it shouldn't be too complicated or it will have less impact and the reader risks getting lost in the detail. For a longer story or novel the plot can be much more complex; you can play with twists and turns, but there must be some convincing resolution at the end.

A series might have a story arc that covers more than one book, resolving the problems of one particular storyline but leaving others that could be taken up in a later title within the series.

You might have sub-plots running alongside the main story-line that weave in and out of the story. Beware that they don't take the reader completely away from the main story; a sub-plot should enhance but never take over from the main storyline.

It can be useful to look at your plot in the form of a flow chart. Try picking out the main plot points and see where the sub-plots link into them. This also helps you identify where the climax of your story arrives, and if it is close enough to the end to keep the reader guessing and interested. One writer I know creates her plot in the shape of a circle and writes in various plot points like the minutes on a clock face.

If you get stuck at some point in your story, looking back at the original plot and at how you constructed it can help get you back on track. Perhaps it will show where the flaws are that are holding you up.

If you are not keen on working out the plot beforehand, you would do well to ask yourself a few questions as you write. This applies even if by then you are in the final revision stage of your book.

- Is the storyline holding together logically, or are elements of the story stretched to make it work? This will throw the story out of shape.
- Are all the sub-plots resolved and not left hanging unfinished?
- Is the story evenly told throughout the book or is it slow to start and then in a rush at the end?

- Is the pace of the story working for *you*, making the best use of drawing out the suspense and rattling on in action scenes?
- Is the final climax of the story expected; does it get resolved in a credible fashion?

It's easy to be enticed into taking the easy route when solving one of your character's problems. Make sure you don't try to solve problems in a totally unrealistic or illogical way, making the ending feel contrived. Never patronise or underestimate your young reader.

Pace

A story should progress at whatever pace you decide suits the tale. There will be times when it rushes forward excitedly, and others when it needs to be slower and more stretched out. You may find that your story gains pace as you get further into it and grow in confidence, becoming more at home with your characters. Be aware of that when you look at the plot, and try not to rush through the finale because you know you are close to finishing the book. You might want to go back and rewrite an earlier part when you see the story in its entirety at the revision stage; perhaps you understand the story or characters better and realise that the pace is not doing all it can for the plot.

There will be times in your story when you want to make it move faster because it is reaching some kind of climax, or conflict. It may be because you want to create a sense of excitement or movement. One way to achieve this is by writing in a slightly breathless way, with short staccato sentences and vocabulary that expresses a sense of urgency or even fear. Any book would be exhausting to read if you kept this up for its entirety; it would also lose its effect, so it needs to be tempered with slower sections.

You may also want to slow the story to create a sense of anticipation by tempting the reader with snippets of information, making them wait to discover the answer to a problem or question but not giving too much away until you are ready.

Longer sentences with more descriptive language can be helpful in slowing the pace. There are no hard and fast rules, but you might look at how other authors have used pace to the benefit of their storytelling and try to find ways to vary the pace that suit your particular style of writing.

> Give your main character a problem and keep the readers guessing as he/she tries to solve it. **Julia Jarman**

Sub-plots need to be tied up as you progress through the story. Don't leave them all to the very end, or it will begin to feel like a list of solutions. Beware of leaving any sub-plot unresolved: if you do there is a risk that the reader will be left feeling unsatisfied and wondering what happened, which will give the sub-plot more importance than it was meant to have. Ultimately this can spoil the ending, because the reader is left waiting to see what you have done with some minor character or plot line.

Exercise 1

Have a look at a children's book of similar length to the one you are writing. See if you can take apart the layout of the plot (this can be useful practice for getting to grips with writing a synopsis and analysing your own writing structure). Where does the story begin? What are the main plot points? Here is an example of one way you could do this, using Cinderella and a sub-plot of the ugly sisters' story.

- **Plot**
  - **Sub-plot**
- Cinderella's father dies and she is miserable. Her wicked stepmother takes over the house, making her a servant.
  - step-sisters look for ways to make her life a misery
- Cinderella meets prince by chance.
  - step-sisters hear the Prince is looking for a bride and squabble over which of them will marry him
- Her step-mother tells Cinderella she is not allowed to go to the ball and has to work in the kitchen.
  - step-sisters tell Cinderella to make them dresses for the ball

- Cinderella is making a mess of the dresses but her Fairy God-mother arrives and, using magic, finishes the dresses for her.
  - step-sisters tell Cinderella the beautiful dresses are only just suitable and leave for the ball
- The Fairy Godmother arranges for Cinderella to go to the ball.
  - step-sisters try to woo the prince and Cinderella arrives but no one recognises her
- Prince dances with Cinderella
  - step-sisters are being ignored; they are jealous
- Cinderella has to leave at midnight and loses her slipper.
- Prince searches for a foot to fit the slipper.
  - step-sisters try to fit into the slipper and fight over it
- Prince finds Cinderella and asks to marry her.
  - Cinderella tells her step-mother & step-sisters they can come and work in the palace
- Cinderella and the prince live happily ever after.

Exercise 2

Take your own story, or another you know well or have read recently. Sum up the story in three sentences. What is it about?

Write a short synopsis of the story, no more than a page. Identify whose story it is, what it's about, and summarise the major plot points, climax and final resolution.

Exercise 3

Now that you have your plot, list your main characters, giving a very brief description of who they are and their relationship to each other.

13.

Characters

Character creates story. I can have lots of ideas that would make a good story, but it's only when I put a character into that situation and see how they would react that it begins to move, take shape – the character is writing the story for you. The most exciting feeling you can imagine! **Catherine MacPhail**

Your characters are what makes your story come alive. If you can get your reader to care about the characters, they will want to find out what happens to them and from that moment on you have a story that children will want to read.

The wonderful thing about writing for children is that your characters can be anything imaginable. They can be children, of any age; they might be creatures – real animals, insects or imaginary fantasy creatures; they might even be inanimate objects that you bring to life.

When creating your characers, do bear in mind the age of the children you are writing for. Children generally like to read about characters that are, or appear to be, of a similar age to themselves – or a year or two older. They are rarely interested in stories where the main characters are adults or even children who are much older than they are. One of the reasons a story is appealing is that you can place yourself in the position of the main character(s). That is not going to work if your characters are so much older that the child cannot relate to them.

You make your characters live and breathe by giving them emotions, fears and hopes, weaknesses and strengths. If the reader becomes emotionally involved with a character, they will care about what happens to them. When your reader starts to care, you have them hooked.

It's useful if you can *picture* your character, get to know them and get a feel for their personality. Even if some of what you know about them never ends up on the page, you have to know and understand how they will react in a given situation. If you don't know your characters well enough they will seem like cardboard cut-outs and will never engage the reader.

Not all of your characters have to be fully fleshed out. Don't name all your minor characters or give too much detail about them. Minor characters should stay that way, but your main characters have to be recognisable. They need to have lives, problems, hopes and aspirations, much the same as we have. We have to laugh and cry with them, experience their love, hate, fear, jealousy, embarrassment and any other relevant emotion.

How to create a character

Most characters do not fall fully formed into your head; they develop gradually. You might want to use an animal or other creature, or even an inanimate object as a character.

Vivian French has created a wonderful character, Gubble, in her book *Robe of Skulls*. Gubble is described as having been in service to the sorceress Lady Lamora for 170 years. He has a flat green face, lives in a dark cupboard and speaks in an endearingly comical way. He waddles and is constantly worried about 'Trouble' coming his way. He even sucks his thumb. These details are cleverly introduced a little at a time so that a picture emerges and the reader gets a real sense of the character's personality. As a result, you care what happens to him.

Sometimes, in a book for younger children you may want to place your young character in a potentially dangerous or difficult situation – such as being out alone at night. In this case it can be better to use a character that is not human, hence removing the danger slightly from the child and making the situation less frightening.

Whatever you decide, the things that make a character real to the reader are its likes and dislikes, its faults and virtues, and most of all its emotional responses and the emotional response it generates – both in the characters around it and in the reader.

So how do you create a credible character that someone will care about?

> Before I start writing I make a list of characters and put down as many details about them that I can think of: age, colour of hair, height, nature (fiery, docile, argumentative), where they live, relationships with each other. They begin to build up in my head. Then I am ready to begin. **Joan Lingard**

You need to get to know your character well enough to be able to anticipate their reaction in any given situation without really thinking about it. Take Cinderella's wicked stepmother: would she have given Cinderella the night off to go to the ball? Perhaps she would have bought a lovely gown for Cinderella to wear? Our natural reaction is, 'No, she would never do any of these things!' We know what kind of person she is, what her motives are, and how she would react in that situation.

Similarly you need to get to know your character's quirks, likes and dislikes so that this knowledge can inform your writing and the storyline as it relates to that character. There are various ways to create a character, and most of these are just ways of getting to know them well enough for them to appear real when you tell their story.

Think about the details of their appearance, and about how they see themselves. Are they tidy, well dressed or scruffy? Are they always clean or always dirty? Is appearance important to them or do they not care at all? This will naturally lead to further considerations. What matters to them, and what do they want most? Who do they care about or want to impress, or worry about disappointing? What are they scared of?

You may want to create an 'anchor' for your character – something that makes them memorable to the reader. This could be achieved by giving them an interesting name, possibly even something that suggests the opposite of their nature. You could link them with a sensory impression, such as a particular smell/scent or a sound. Perhaps you can hear the way they walk or something they always carry; a stick rattling on railings, or a habit such as biting their nails or drumming their fingers.

Their manner of speech often fixes a character in your head and can reveal a lot about them. It could be the particular rhythm of their speech, or a phrase or word that they like to use often. It could be because of where they have been brought up or their social class.

When introducing characters, it's important to make them either visually or emotionally memorable to your reader. Consider how difficult it is to remember a group of people you have never met before, if you are introduced to them one after the other. If they are particularly nasty or different or quirky you have a reason to remember them.

You may have a reason to link their name or appearance with some previous knowledge. This is easier with visual clues: we may recall someone because they wore a large silly hat, looked particularly tall or short or were otherwise physically distinctive.

Avoid long descriptions and bringing in too many characters at the same time. You may have spent a lot of time creating these characters, but although you know them well your reader will not easily cope with too much information at one time. When you introduce a character they should make some impact, so that when they appear again the reader doesn't find themselves asking, 'Susan? Who was that?'

Don't have too many characters, either. The temptation can be to have a grand cast, but it will be difficult to keep them organised in your reader's mind and even more difficult to make them all sufficiently distinctive.

An interesting technique is to introduce one character through the perceptions of another. Invite the reader to strive to see beyond this particular character's motives or lack of sensitivity to the new character; try introducing a question in the reader's mind about everything the original character says, so that they realise their view might be skewed. The reader becomes involved and it gives them pause for thought. They may recognise that the narrator-character is mistaken, angry or jealous.

People aren't all good or bad. Don't make the mistake of thinking that children can't cope with bad or unhappy people. Children have a great capacity for empathy. **Joanna Kenrick**

This can be done very simply but to great effect in a picture book, by using a statement made by the character that is completely altered in the reader's perception by what is seen in the illustrations. An excellent example of this is *The Man on the Moon* by Simon Bartram, where the main character is convinced that there are no such things as aliens. We, however, can see from the pictures that there are aliens all around him; he just hasn't noticed them. Even very young children can see the humour in this, and as they are not reading the words their attention is all on the images, which can carry a different message for them to spot.

Exercise 1

Try using a spider diagram to help you consider what aspects of your character you might want to think about. Try placing four on one page as below:

VISUAL
(What does the character look like?
Clothes, hair, height, build)

ACTIONS
(How does the character move?
Fast/ jerky/ ponderous)

EMOTIONS
(Think about emotions your character
might display or hide)

SPEECH
(Does your character's speech highlight
class/upbringing/geographical origins or
an impediment?)

Exercise 2

Think about five things your character might wear. Describe each item in detail, considering if it is old or new, its colour and texture, and what the character thinks of it. Do they like it, or do they have another reason for wearing it? How does it make them feel?

Exercise 3

Write a description of your character and embed it within a story, but make it interesting. Don't give too much description at one time; break it up to make it flow more smoothly. This allows the reader to absorb the information more naturally.

The straw rustled and out of the middle of it a triangular head appeared. Above the muzzle two large brown eyes stared at me, unblinking.

"Oh, she's gorgeous! Hello, Veritas, I'm Kate."

With much shuffling and a shake of her head the baby wyvern shrugged off the last of the straw and waddled towards me rather unsteadily, its tiny wings fluttering.

Exercise 4

Create a couple of characters from inanimate objects and use them to suggest a story. Let your imagination go wild in this exercise.

Start with one object (e.g. a garden rake) and make a list of its characteristics. What does it look like (tall, short, large feet, long green hair, etc.). What does it like/dislike (likes riding a motorbike, hopes to go to the moon one day, proud and lazy, dislikes having to work in the garden and getting dirty)? What kind of temperament (easily upset by personal comments but is inclined to make rude comments about others, so has few friends and is lonely)? Give your character a name.

Now create another character from something completely different (e.g. a shy, fearful suitcase). Do the same with this character but make sure it's quite different from the first one. Find a place or reason why they are forced into each other's company (perhaps they are put in a box in a garage when they learn they are about to be thrown away at the rubbish dump and need to make a bid for freedom), and see what reaction this will cause. In this way you create the essential conflict in your story: what might happen between them, and how they would react to the situation. Would they help each other or just squabble?

14.

Dialogue

One of the most important parts of a story is the dialogue. How your characters speak, the rhythm of their speech and how they interact with each other reveals more about who they are and what they think than almost anything else.

To write good dialogue you need to listen to the way children talk to each other – on the bus, in the playground, in a shop. What they say and how they say it (and often what they *don't* say) defines who they are. They will speak differently to adults than they will to other children, but don't fall into the trap of trying to write dialogue copied exactly from actual speech. Just as any detective story will not tell you blow by blow all the boring routine jobs that are involved in any police investigation, good dialogue will try to capture the feeling of real speech without the ums, ahs or 'hesitation and repetition' people use when speaking.

Listen to the pace of speech when someone is excited or upset, and consider how that varies when they are relaxed or unsure of themselves. Try to use this in your writing, to get the reader involved; speech is often more interesting than a page of description. Dialogue can be charged with emotion, whether suppressed or explosive, or possibly with just an underlying threat.

'Oh my goodness! When I was young the doctor would have been called if anyone had finger nails that colour,' Mrs Beal said in mock horror. 'Would have been fun, though,' her eyes twinkled. 'I hear your mother is coming to visit next week,' she continued, hardly stopping for breath.

I watched as Beth's face drained of colour. After a moment or two Mrs Beal carried on, oblivious to the effect her words were having on Beth.

'We'll have to get the place spic and span before she comes, won't we?'

Beth got up and ran out of the room.

Mrs. Beal turned back to wipe the table, 'Oh! Where's Beth gone, dear? Was it the door?' She shrugged, 'I didn't hear anything.'

You might want to break up long passages of speech by having you character involved in some occupation, interweaving their actions with completely unrelated dialogue. It could be something as simple as having a child discussing a problem while they are writing: the way in which they write, perhaps digging into the paper or idly doodling, can help to reveal their emotional response to the conversation.

It's usually not a good idea to try to write in dialect; this can make reading the dialogue difficult. However, the odd word or phrase, a character's rhythm of speech, or even the order words are used in, can suggest a particular origin, ethnic background or social stratum. Don't do this with a heavy hand, though, or it will just seem ridiculous.

While it's important to know who is speaking, too many 'he said' or 'she saids' can break up the flow of dialogue and annoy the reader. The same can be said for the use of adverbs: 'he said blankly' (or stupidly, or hesitantly) will not be as effective as replacing the adverb with action or interaction between characters. Remember to 'show and not tell'. You may have heard this before and it is such good advice to keep at the back of your mind when you are writing. It simply means that instead of telling your reader that a character did, felt or said something, you show it in the way they behave. Show the character's motivations and reactions; don't tell the reader that s/he is sad and saying something sadly but rather show it in his or her expression, actions or actual words used. This technique can be very subtle and you do have to work a little harder to make it effective. I usually find that at the end of a spell of writing, when I am getting tired, I tend to get lazy and often have to go back and change sections where I have just told – not shown – the reader what I wanted them to know.

So for example, rather than say 'he said, worriedly' you might show the character's anxiety through some small action – biting a lip, nervously tapping a nail or tail against a surface, pulling at their fringe, or fiddling with the hem of a shirt or skirt. This can become a particular trait of that character and thus add to their overall believability:

> Jenny had been crying and she wondered nervously if her father was angry with her.
> *becomes*
> As Jenny looked up at her father's face, searching for a sign of bad temper, she was unconsciously shredding the tissue he had given her to wipe away her tears.

Alternatively you might use dialogue: instead of telling the reader that the character likes chocolate, it can come out in the dialogue as follows:

> 'Let's go to the shop and get some chocolate,' Gina licked her lips. 'Warm, smooth chocolate. Peel off the wrapper and break off a chunk ... mmmmm!'

Common sense will tell you to use this method sparingly. Although it can add to your story, be careful not to slow up the pace of the action with too much description. You have to use your own judgement, but this is often where a good editor, agent or course tutor can give you advice.

At times a simple 'she said', used sparingly, can be better than trying to think of different ways to say it on every line. You don't want your character 'gasping' or 'giggling' their way through the dialogue! Use these kind of verbs with caution; often in dialogue, if it's obvious who is speaking, you can eradicate the 's/he saids' altogether. Read your work out loud and you will immediately see where the writing becomes lumpy and needs to be refined. If you are timid about doing this, try to find a time when you are alone or behind closed doors.

Remember that layout makes dialogue easier to read. Indent your speech and use a new line for each new person speaking. If you are not sure about how to lay out your dialogue to best effect, there are plenty of good books which will guide you through any difficulties with punctuation. The Collins Little Gem is one of my favourites if I want to check something specific, and *Eats, Shoots and Leaves* by Lynne Truss makes grammar easy to read about.

Exercise 1

Take two characters – you could use ones you made up earlier – and write the dialogue between them when one suspects the other of keeping a secret from them.

Think about who they are and how they would feel in this situation. Is the secret something dreadful or a nice surprise, and how does the discussion or argument end? When you have finished, try reading your dialogue out loud – or you might persuade someone else to read one of the characters and seek their opinion.

Exercise 2

Try writing a monologue where the character speaking is occupied in some task. They might be doing something ordinary, such as cleaning out a pet's cage or combing out another character's hair, or it could be something much more unusual – some craft or special skill. This has various benefits, because you can show the speaker's emotional reaction through their actions while at the same time describing in an interesting and textural way some special occupation. Breaking your description up with dialogue – this could be the character recalling a previous conversation – will prevent you from boring your reader with too much detail.

15.

POV (Point of View)

Keep true to the deep 'point of view' of your child character, and definitely not from the point of view of an amused, all-knowing adult observer. Competitions and agencies are awash with unpublishable manuscripts where that sneaky adult point of view came creeping in and dominated the writing and the story.

Penny Dolan

The point of view is really just when you ask yourself whose story it is, and who is telling it. There are various ways of using POV and each brings a different style to the story.

Third-person Point of View

You might want to be a narrator and tell the story from the outside – perhaps the most common and the easiest way to tell a story.

Example
Once upon a time there were three Billy Goats Gruff ...

Using the narrator method leaves you free to concentrate on your characters and the plot, rather than worrying about the more technical aspects of the POV.

You may start your story and decide later that it would work better if you changed the POV. It can be interesting to see how much this can change the focus, but always be consistent and make sure you don't slip from one POV to another unintentionally.

First-person Point of View

You might want the main character to tell the story in their own voice and from their own viewpoint and opinion.

Example

My name is Grufflet. I live with my two older brothers and most of the folk in our village call us the Billy Goats Gruff ...

The main benefit of first-person POV is that your reader is immediately involved in the story and the action from a personal angle. However, if the action is happening away from that character, you get only what they have had reported to them, rather than an 'on the spot' version.

A further drawback with this method is that the reader only sees what the main character sees, hears and thinks, and everything in the story is seen from their POV. The use of 'I' has to be tempered with other ways of beginning sentences so that it's not endlessly repetitive.

You can do various other things with this viewpoint. For example, when the main character doesn't believe what another character is saying, it's possible to make the reader realise that the main character is blinkered in their ideas. This can be done either in a humorous way or to create tension. At times it can make the reader want to shout 'look behind you!' or 'don't believe him!' because you know that the main character is not seeing the whole story or is trying to believe that someone is good and kind when the reader begins to suspect – then becomes convinced – that the character is being misled. In Rebecca Lisle's *Curse of Toads*, which is told in the third person but mainly through the main character's eyes, the author uses this well. We see that Reuben is inclined to think the best of the strange Dr Flyte, partly because he is tired and Dr Flyte is kind to him. But as the story progresses, more of Dr Flyte's character and motivations are revealed. Although Reuben suspects him at times, the reader catches on much more quickly.

Multiple Point of View

Occasionally a story might be told using multiple viewpoints – i.e. seeing the story from the viewpoint of various different characters. This might take the form of each chapter being written from a different character's POV. If you choose this method, avoid using too many different characters as it can become confusing to the reader.

When using multiple viewpoints it is essential for each character to sound quite different in the way that they think, speak and act or react. If they don't, the reader will become confused because all the characters sound the same. Multiple POV can be very difficult to do successfully and for that reason is not particularly advisable for the novice writer.

> Point of view can cause problems – it's something that editors keep an eagle eye out for. Multiple points of view make editors uneasy. They would really rather you stick with your main character, whom they expect to be a child. If you choose to stray from this, at least be sure you know when you're doing it.
>
> **Sue Purkiss**

Exercise 1
Look at some books for children and see what the POV is. Look at a book written from the first-person POV and see how the writer has handled it. How have they told the story?

Exercise 2
Try rewriting a paragraph or two of the story from a different POV – either the narrator's or in the first person. This exercise will help you see what the differences are, and how the various viewpoints can alter the way in which the story is told. Try to avoid too much use of the word 'I', especially at the beginning of sentences.

16.

Beginnings and Endings

Beginnings

Beginnings are important. One must catch the attention of the reader on the first page, so start when the actual story starts and don't indulge in detailed descriptions of the characters, or what has happened to them beforehand. That can come out as the story progresses.

Joan Lingard

So you have an idea, you know your characters, and you've thought carefully about the plot. Where do you actually *begin*? There are no rules: you can begin your story anywhere you want ... but if you find that you are stumped trying to come up with an amazing beginning that will astound your readers, stop right there.

Don't get hung up on writing the best possible beginning so that you go over it again and again and get no further than the first page. Just start writing. Although beginnings are very important, at this stage it's not quite so important how you start your story because when you get to the revision stage you may decide that you want to begin in a different place to give your story more impact.

Get a picture in your head of what is happening and put it down on paper. It's often easier to change and mould your story once you have got it started, rather than staring at that dreaded blank page. This is discussed further in the chapter on revision (*see* pp. 99–105).

When considering your beginning, one thing to keep in mind is that children, especially younger children, don't want a long and drawn-out beginning; this will often make them lose interest. Unlike adults, few children will read a book 'just because they started it'. Most will discard anything that doesn't capture their interest immediately.

Rather than focusing on how to start, think more widely about the best way to tell your story. Perhaps you *do* want to start at the very beginning, drawing your reader in with an intriguing first page.

Bill's New Frock by Anne Fine does this incredibly well. It introduces Bill, a young boy who wakes up one morning to discover that he is a girl. Before he has time to consider what this means his mum comes in and suggests he wears a pink dress. This introduces the main character but also leaves questions in the reader's mind.

Try to draw an emotional response from the reader from the very first scene, so that they will feel engaged immediately with the characters and the plot, and be curious to read on and find out more.

Another option might be to start in the middle of some action; your character or characters may be running, fighting or in the middle of an argument. Make it exciting. After the action slows down you can fill in some of the background, gradually answering some of the reader's questions while continuing the story.

Alternatively you may want to start the story in the middle of a discussion or argument between your characters. Through dialogue, you can give a background to the characters' personalities and situation – and often, more is understood by what is *not* said, as by what is expressed.

Starting at the end of a story – at the dramatic climax where everything seems to be at its worst point for your character – is probably a better choice for the older, more confident reader. They will be able to follow the story as you backtrack from what is almost the finale, filling in what has gone before to get them to this point, and then satisfying their curiosity as to how your character resolves the problem.

Remember to keep the story going with action and dialogue, and don't fall into the trap of telling too much, rather than showing what is happening. I think it's useful if you can visualise your story as a film rolling in your head as you write it. This will help to keep it visual and moving.

Often, fairy tales or folktales are retold in different ways. For example, you could start *Cinderella* at the beginning, with the return from her father's funeral. You could set the scene as sombre and frightening, when our heroine realises that her wicked stepmother has decided to make her a servant to the family.

Or you might want to start the story in the middle, when Cinders is feeling miserable about having made a complete mess of her step-sister's dresses, just before her Fairy godmother arrives. The story could equally be told from another character's point of view: perhaps years later, an old palace retainer is remembering how Cinderella first met her prince. In this way the same story can be approached from different beginnings.

To keep the reader interested and wanting to turn the page, you must keep them guessing – even with an old familiar tale where the reader knows what will happen in the end. It's *how* you tell it that is important.

To sum up, then, start off your story by creating questions in your reader's mind. This will keep them engrossed, wanting to find out the answers. Introduce your main character(s) quickly and interestingly; starting off with a minor character can backfire on you if they become more interesting than the main character and then fade into the background. The child reader will wonder why, and where they have gone, taking the interest away from where you want the story to go.

Exercise 1

Take a story you know and try writing the beginning – just the first couple of paragraphs – in different ways. Remember to create questions in the reader's mind, and that the beginning has to capture the interest of your reader and make them want to read on to find out what happens. Try the following:

- Begin with an atmospheric introduction leading into the start of the story.
- Start in the middle of some action or dialogue between characters.

- Start just before the climax of the story, re-telling what brought the character(s) to that point.

Endings

> Keep the tension rising right up to the end, then let your protag-onist solve the problem in a surprising way.
>
> **Julia Jarman**

How you end your story will depend very much upon the way in which you have told it: the *structure*. You need to make sure that after the climactic point, when potentially everything has gone wrong for your main character, you find a credible solution to the problem that is not simplistic. This will give your reader a sense of satisfaction, even if the outcome is not what the character wanted or hoped for at the beginning.

You need to provide answers to all of the reader's questions, and when writing for children it's especially important that your story ends with some sense of optimism. Children want to know that life will go on, and that some kind of a solution is possible to most situations.

> Everyone should come to the right 'end'. It's not just a question of loose ends; it's also a question of reader satisfaction. The reader needs to feel encouraged and hopeful for their own future.
>
> **Joanna Kenrick**

The end of your story should never leave the reader feeling cheated (i.e. 'it was all a dream'). It should come full circle from the beginning, so that the reader has a sense that they have come to the end of a journey with the characters, or resolved an issue that was the reason for the story when it began. A story might end leaving a slight hint that there is more to tell (perhaps in a sequel), but even if that is the case, each story should still be able to stand on its own.

Exercise

Look at some books you have read for different age groups, paying particular attention to what the writer has chosen to write in the last page or chapter. Think about how that makes you feel in the context of the rest of the story. Has it left you feeling hopeful for the future of the characters? Would you have written it differently?

> I have always wanted to know what happens in any story, especially ones I have begun. **Caroline Pitcher**

17.

Settings and Visualisation

To make your reader believe in your story, you need to create a credible world or 'setting' for your characters. Without the visual input provided by film, you must create the texture of the setting with words that stimulate the senses of your reader – without them realising you are doing it. To create your setting you need to provide all the stimuli the reader would experience if they were in the situation your character is in. Try to practise this by thinking of all the five senses: sight – touch – smell – hearing – taste. Can you incorporate two of these together, enriching your character's (and therefore your reader's) experience? Think about the screech of an owl swooping down on wide wings at night, or the smell of crumbly rusted iron. Wordy or long descriptions will often make the reader skip ahead, but a few carefully chosen words tied into the story can give it a rich texture.

Try to visualise the scenes you are writing, even if it's just two characters talking in a house. What is around them – what furniture, smells, small sounds? Are there any pets or cars outside? How light or dark is the room? You should have thought about all these details, even if they never make it into the text. If they do, used sparingly they can make the scene more recognisable without being wordy. Consider the clinking of teacups, a cat scratching itself, the sound of wood stretching and groaning in a log cabin.

> I think imagining the book you're writing as a film is helpful in a number of ways. In my recent book I imagined the action from the outset as a series of scenes in a sweeping epic film.
>
> **Sue Purkiss**

Try to make your descriptions original without being weird. Avoid clichés and commonly used sayings or slang, unless they are part of a character's speech. You can link visual extras with memories to give your character background and carry the story along. Here is an example:

> "As the Inspector spoke, I fingered the long furrow gouged out of the chair when Gary had helped us move house. I drew my hand away when he looked at me, as if he could tell that I had been lying when I'd told him Gary had never been here."

Try to see things with a child's eye, as if everything and each experience were brand new. Look for the less obvious details in everyday objects or places. Enjoy using all this wonderful sensory information – but remember to use it sparingly!

Once you have decided on a setting and imagined it visually, remember to be consistent. You can't have a character leave by a second door in a room and later have your characters trapped because there is only one exit.

Like an iceberg, only one-tenth of what the writer knows about the setting and characters should be seen by the reader, but it is that submerged nine-tenths that gives a good story its depth and richness. Long passages of description, however wonderfully they are written, will often bore your child reader. The balance is to give enough imagery and information to create a reality within your story that will entrance and capture your reader, so that they believe they have actually been there with your characters.

Exercise 1

Imagine you are sitting on a chair somewhere you know well. It could be any room in your own house or someone else's; any-where that is familiar to you. Close your eyes and focus on one of your senses at a time. Stop after each one and make short notes on the sounds, smells and tastes you have remembered.

- SOUNDS

  Listen for all the smallest noises we take for granted: Granddad snoring, cat scratching, cars outside, birds singing, trees rustling in the wind, a clock ticking.

- SMELLS

  Try to distinguish any smells in the room as if you had just come in – flowers, furniture polish, pets, wood or perfume.

- TOUCH

  Feel what is around you – the arm of the chair, the seat beneath you, the texture and material, is it comfortable? The shoes/socks against your toes, the clothes you are wearing. What do your clothes feel like from the inside? Are your shoes, belt or neckline too tight or too hot? Beyond that you may have a pet on your lap or someone sitting beside you; how do you know they are there?

- TASTE

  Think of as many different tastes as you can – sweets, chocolate, vinegar, cheese, vegetables, sauces or herbs. Are any of them associated with pleasant or unpleasant memories?

You would never want to use all this information at once, but often we forget how much sensory information we are processing at any moment in time. It is a rich source of material to plunder, but choose carefully and use it sparingly.

Exercise 2

Visualise a character peeling and tasting an orange. Describe it in as much detail as you can, engaging all your senses. Think about the feel and the taste of the skin, the pith and the juices. Describe the smell and the feeling when the rind gets stuck under the character's nails. Is the orange easy or hard to peel? Do they use a knife?

18.

Revision

Revising your work can be just as creative as any other part of the writing process – and it is equally as important. This is the point at which you actually have something to work with. You have written your first draft; now you can hone it, move it around and generally mould it until it is just right.

> Characters, plots, descriptions, etc. are all important – but they're worth nothing at all without feeling and emotion.
>
> **Vivian French**

Conflict and emotion are essential ingredients to any story. Without these there is no story to tell, no reason for the reader to become involved with your characters or plot. At the revision stage you have the opportunity to make the most of any conflict, emotion or situation.

When you revise you should be looking to work up the strengths of a story or a single scene, and to eradicate the weak points. Look out for repetition of particular words or phrases: these can slip in easily without you noticing them, but they can be truly irritating to the reader.

As with other areas of writing, there are no rules about revision: everyone finds their own way of revising. Some prefer to keep on writing until they finish a piece and then go back and revise and edit it all at once. Others revise as they go along. There are pitfalls with the latter, because while you going over and over a piece you have written – perhaps only a chapter, or even a paragraph – you avoid having to face the next part of the story, the next blank page. In doing so you risk making that part of your story so overworked that it loses any freshness it once possessed.

The benefit of using a computer is that when revising you can move great chunks of text or just a few phrases around quite easily. However, remember to save your work frequently when you are typing; there is nothing more demoralising than losing a great piece of writing simply because you have forgotten to save it. Think too about the best way to order your story. You may want to work with the entire story or decide to save it in individual chapters, but always number each draft consecutively – for example, as Story 1, Story 1.1, Story 1.2, and so on. It is a good idea to save previous drafts because you may rewrite something and then decide later that the first draft was actually better. Computers are a fantastic tool for the writer, but being able to revise work so easily can mean you find yourself endlessly revising – never feeling confident enough to say it's done. The resulting story can lose some of its freshness. Some writers email drafts to themselves, so that even if their computer crashes they can still retrieve their original work.

Some people prefer to revise the previous session's writing to get them back into the mood of the piece before continuing. However, you should be aware that it's a prelude, otherwise you may never move out of that comfort zone. It might also be that this piece is not quite right; you may spend a lot of time revising it and later cut it out completely.

When revising, consider the following with care:

- Plot
  - What happens, and when? Is there a question posed close to the start of your story to draw the reader in? Is there a climactic point and where does it come in the story? Is any conflict resolved satisfactorily, and have you tied up all the loose ends?
  - Are your sub-plots woven in through the story? Do they ever take precedence over the main plotline? Are they all resolved?
  - Does the story follow a logical sequence that the reader can follow?
  - Have you made the most of the action or dialogue to emphasise the climactic or exciting passages in the story?

- Characters
  - Are your main characters fully fleshed out, and do we know their strengths and weaknesses, their hopes and desires? Do we see a change in the main character because of what happens during the story? If so, is that change sufficiently clear to the reader?
  - Are any subsidiary characters sufficiently in the background but still original and credible? Have you avoided stereotypes?
  - Do your characters sound consistent in dialogue and/or in attitude?
  - Do they react credibly and consistently with other characters?
- Dialogue
  - Can the reader tell your characters apart by the way they speak?
  - Are the speech patterns of your characters consistent throughout?
  - Does the dialogue further the story or knowledge of the characters?
  - Could your dialogue be shorter, sharper and more revealing?
- Beginning and ending
  - Does your story start in the right place, or would it have more punch or interest if it started at a different point?
  - Does your beginning draw the reader into the story?
  - Does your ending satisfy the reader?
  - Is the ending realistic in terms of the storyline?
- POV (Point of View)
  - Have you told the story from the best POV for maximum effect?
  - Is the POV consistent?
  - If you used the first person, have you varied your sentences to avoid the constant use of 'I'?
- Setting
  - Have you given the reader enough information so that they can visualise every part of the story? Is your setting both credible and consistent?
  - Have you avoided long passages of description, weaving them instead into the action or dialogue?

- Have you made sure any research you have done is used sparingly but effectively?
- Rhyme/rhythm (picture books)
  - If rhyme is used, is it at all forced or does it flow easily, regardless of who is reading it?
  - Does a read-it-aloud story have rhythm so that it's easy to read and listen to? Read it out loud to make sure.
- Punctuation
  - Look carefully at your punctuation and grammar or get someone else to check it for you.

Most writers have little quirks in their writing; one of mine is including too many exclamation marks!!! When I have finished a draft of a piece of work I go through it carefully, taking out the extraneous ones. It's always a good idea to look over your work and see if you have any particular quirks or words or phrases you have used too often. If so, these need to be carefully eradicated, or at least re-thought.

Sometimes a story will need major reconstruction because a character simply does not work. It could be because the character is not credible. If this is the case, you might want to go back to basics and see exactly what you know about them. What are their habits, likes and dislikes, quirks and temperament? If they were to find themselves in a particularly awkward situation, do you know immediately how they would react to it?

If the plot is not holding up try to look at it logically and see what is pulling it out of shape. Sometimes you need to seek help from someone else who could take an objective view and make some constructive suggestions – but if it means a major rewrite because of plot or character faults it can be difficult to accept even the best advice. Always make sure that you are not arguing against the change because it seems like such a huge amount of work to redo it. It is difficult to throw out bits of writing that you particularly like or are proud of, but they might just be the parts that are causing the problem. Time spent fixing these kinds of flaws, while daunting, can make your story gripping and memorable. If you are still stuck, try putting your work away for a while – even for a couple of months – and coming to it fresh when you are not so close to it.

If you have corrected any major flaws and honed the structure and character of the story, now is the time to make it shine by going back over the words and phrases to see where you can polish it still further. Take out any extra words that affect the flow. Try reading a part or all of it out loud, even if it is meant to be read silently. You may at some time be asked to read out a passage or all of a short story, so this is good practice – but it's also amazing what you can discover that had not been obvious on the printed page. Repetition that the eye skims over becomes more obvious when read out loud, and this gives you a chance to change it. Errors in pace, rhythm and emphasis also stand out. The spoken word reveals a lot – try it and see.

> As a writer you can get too close to your work; adore it, revere it. Not good. You need to take a few steps away from it. That's why I always 'compost' my work. I put it away and let it mature for at least a couple of weeks – even though I am desperate to send it straight to my agent. Then I take another look at it and all the terrible faults jump out and I can fix them.
>
> Rebecca Lisle

Writing courses and writing groups

You may feel that you need some personal advice on your writing, or a way to get regular feedback on your work. If so, you could consider joining a local writing group – or even starting your own. This can also be a good way of meeting other people who are interested in writing.

Writing groups can take different forms. Some are run by local libraries and may feature visits from a 'writer in residence' (a published writer who works part-time with writing groups or other people in the community). You can find out about these groups by asking at your local library or looking online. There are national associations such as NAWG (National Association of Writers' Groups), which covers all areas of the UK; in Scotland there is also the Scottish Association of Writers' Groups (SAW). Their websites are given at the back of this book. The

BBC 'Get Writing' site also lists writers' groups. Members meet to discuss writing and share their work with each other. Some groups are more active than others, but the main thing is to find the kind of group that operates in a way to suit you.

It might be useful to discover if the group you are considering joining has members who are writing for children. This doesn't mean that you have to avoid groups where no one else is interested in writing for children, but it is good to ask the question before you decide.

Arts Councils and other agencies sometimes offer special opportunities, including bursaries, for the novice writer. See the final section of this book for details about where to find such information.

You may be interested in a distance-writing course that operates by post and has a series of assignments to work through with a tutor who will comment on your work and offer advice. There are also evening classes in creative writing, or you might want to enrol on one of the diploma or degree courses in creative writing run by colleges or universities. There are some writing courses and centres listed in the Information section of this book.

Another option is attending a short residential course, such as the Arvon Foundation creative writing courses. These run for five days with a group of about 16 writers tutored by two professional writers, and are great opportunities for obtaining expert advice. They also enable you to spend time on your own writing while discussing writing with others of a like mind. Arvon's courses attract both published and unpublished writers seeking a brief respite from the distractions of home and family, and are well worth the investment of both time and money.

> If you want to be a writer, you have to get used to spending a lot of time sitting by yourself, facing the page or screen. Your family and friends may need to get used to this writing time, too. It isn't always easy or very sociable, and you will have to find ways of managing real life and writing life. **Penny Dolan**

Publishers and agents are under pressure these days, with less and less to time to spend doing editorial work. The closer your manuscript is to being publishable when you submit it, the more chance it will have of being accepted.

Not everyone wants to join a group or take a course, and you may want one-to-one help with your writing. When you have something that you think is ready for publication, you might decide to consider one of the literary advisory agencies, who will give you a critique on your work and advice on how to continue. These agencies will charge you a fee to read and critique your work. Most will offer you a report on your manuscript, varying in length, detail and price; you can find out more about such agencies by looking at their websites.

These websites tend to be very positive and encouraging, and usually include the names of the successful writers who have benefited from the company's help. This can sometimes make it seem like an easy route to success, but there is no such thing. It is worth remembering that every success arises from a mixture of talent and hard work. There is no magic formula, and there are no guarantees.

> It's very important to bear in mind what you are actually paying a manuscript agency for. It's not for a quick leg-up to a publisher or agent; it's to have your manuscript assessed. Yes, on very rare occasions an agency will place an exceptional manuscript with an agent, but what the vast majority of new authors most need is a good editor to go over their work.
>
> **Terry Edge** (Freelance editor and writing coach)

Many authors give writing tips on their websites, and you will find some excellent information there. The website of the SAS (Scattered Authors' Society) is a good place to find links to children's authors' websites, together with a host of other information from a wide variety of authors who write for children of all ages and in all genres.

> Young readers won't put up with all that claptrap about writing being torture. They expect you to enjoy it, or to get out and do something else. **Eleanor Updale**

Section 3
Submissions to a Publisher or Agent

19.

Introduction

You can never be sure that anyone's going to like your next story enough to publish it. Oh, the thrill when they do ...!

Valerie Wilding

There are no sure-fire ways to get published, but there are things you can do to make sure that your work is considered seriously by a publisher or agent and not discarded at the first opportunity.

Unfortunately it's a fact that publishers and agents are looking for reasons to reject your work. This is not because they don't want to read it, but rather because they are generally swamped by so many submissions that they need to do some sort of weeding out. Therefore it's *your* job to ensure that your work is in the 'this looks promising' pile!

When you have worked on your manuscript until you feel it's the very best it can be, you need to apply the same stringent efforts to the processes of preparing and submitting it. In this way you can be confident that it has the best possible chance. Remember that this is your calling card, and the first impression will count. So make it a good one.

20.

How to Prepare Your Manuscript

No one is going to take your work seriously if you don't make the effort to prepare and present it properly. A handwritten manuscript is just not acceptable these days; nor is anything that looks as if it has been read and re-read with dog-eared pages, coffee stains or the reek of cigarette smoke. This is understandable when you think of how many submissions publishers and agents receive; they want something that is going to be easy to read and pleasant to handle.

Some golden rules of presentation

- Check your manuscript thoroughly for grammar, spelling and careless errors.
- Use single sheets of A4 white paper, and keep them clean.
- Print on one side only.
- Double-space the text.
- Don't use a fancy font or a small one; point 12–14 is best.
- Don't justify the text on the right.
- Leave good margins on both sides of the text.
- Make sure your dialogue starts on a new line and is indented.
- Number the pages consecutively. Don't start at 1 with each new chapter; if you absolutely have to add a page, number it (e.g. 16, 16a).
- Start each chapter on a new page.
- Start the text of each chapter a few lines further down from the chapter title or number.
- If possible include a header with your name and book title on each page.

- Don't clip the pages together with paperclips or staples, or bind them in a fancy binder. Most publishers and agents would prefer single sheets held together with an elastic band, or one around the middle and another at right angles if it's required.
- Send a cover page with title and contact details (*see* below for an example).
- Never send out a dog-eared copy – print a fresh one.
- Keep a copy, it might get lost in the post!
- Send in a short covering letter (*see* page 112 for an example).
- Always send return postage (SAE).

Sample front cover page

Contact details here
    Name
    Address
    Postcode
    Telephone/mobile
    Email
    Website (if relevant)

TITLE
by
Name (or pen name)

short description can go here
(i.e. Picture book
OR a short novel for 6–9 yr olds)

(number of words)   (copyright symbol – your name/year)
Approx 6000 words   © A.N. Author 2008

Synopsis and cover letter

Normally you would send a publisher or agent the first few chapters and a synopsis of your story, unless it is very short or a picture book, in which case you send the full story. Always send the first consecutive chapters – never an odd selection. From the chapters they will judge how well you can write, and the synopsis should give them the bones of your story: who the main characters are, what happens to them and how the story is resolved.

Remember that a synopsis is not like the blurb you find at the back of a book, the purpose of which is to entice someone to pick it up and buy it. Instead the synopsis enables an editor or agent to judge whether your storyline is working, if your plot is sound, and if it looks like the plot points will be resolved in a logical manner at the end, including any twists and turns. For that reason it's important to make your synopsis follow the storyline just as the reader would, together with any surprises, twists and turns as they would occur in the story. Try not to make your synopsis quite as long as the book!

With your package all ready to go, you need to send it to the right person. Do some research as to whom you should contact, and make sure you find out the full and correct name of the editor or agent. This is really important: don't irriate your recipient by failing to spell their name correctly.

Some individuals will prefer submissions by email and others as hard copy sent by post. *Always* send a covering letter giving some information about your writing background and any publications. Make sure that this information is relevant, concise and accurate. Don't ever say that your family or friends have loved your stories; the agent/or publisher has no interest in their opinion. However, they might be interested if another published writer or publishing professional has expressed an interest.

State any particular skills or experience you may have that are relevant – i.e. for writing educational books if you have been a teacher, or if your book is non-fiction and you have a relevant occupation.

Describe the basis of your story in a couple of sentences, but keep the letter short. They may want to know something about you, but in the end the writing is what will sell – not a letter giving your life history.

Sample cover letter

Contact details here
Name
Address
Postcode
Telephone/mobile
Email
Website (if relevant)

Dear (name of editor/agent)

Please find enclosed the first three chapters and a synopsis of **** (Name of your book or story here) which I feel would fit well in your list, and with your (XXXX) imprint, in particular.

**** is an historical adventure story set in 16th-century northern Europe. Martha is young servant girl who thinks she is worthless and timid, but who is driven by the desire for revenge after her family is murdered. With the help of Johann, a young innkeeper's son, she discovers she is capable of much more than she had ever imagined.

I have enclosed an SAE for return postage should you feel that my work is not suitable for your list.

Yours sincerely
A.N. Author

21.

Where and How to Send Your Work

When trying to decide where to send your work, you can look for likely agents and publishers in the *Children's Writers' and Artists' Yearbook* or *The Writer's Handbook Guide to Writing for Children*. Ask at your local bookshop or library for a current edition.

Use your research to make sure the publisher publishes the right kind of children's books. There is no point in sending a picture book to a publisher who specialises in teenage novels, or a children's book to a publisher who does not publish children's books at all. Look in a good children's bookshop at the imprint pages of books of a similar kind or age level, where you will find the name and usually the contact details of the publisher.

Be sure to look at the © sign beside the author's name and the date that follows it (i.e. © Linda Strachan 2008). This will tell you how long ago the book was written and how up to date the information about the publisher is. Even if it is a later edition it will show the original copyright date and the original publisher as well as the current one, but it's always a good idea to check that the address and contact details are up to date.

Be aware that there are trends in publishing, so that publishers may not publish the same kind and style of books or storylines today as they did ten or 20 years ago. Call them up and ask for the name of the editor who deals with a particular type of book or imprint. Don't ask to speak to the editor, but you can ask them to send you their latest catalogue, which will tell you where your book would fit within their list. You can mention the imprint in your cover letter, which shows them that you have taken the time to research it and that you know what they are currently publishing.

Even if you prepare what seems like the perfect submission, you still may not meet with success. You might eventually decide to consider another route to publication – such as self-publishing.

Vanity publishing

Vanity publishing is a term you may have heard and been warned about. What is it? A vanity publisher will offer to publish your book at a cost to you: this means that you pay them and they publish your book. It may seem like a good idea, particularly if you have had some rejections from mainstream publishers, but there are associated problems. Many such companies don't care whether the book is any good; they are out to make money from you. To get it they may make all kinds of promises, which will usually vanish into thin air – like your money.

Vanity publishers are not likely to do any editing or proof-reading, and some will not do any layout work either, relying on you to provide the manuscript 'printer ready'. The results can be difficult to read and contain many errors.. Their profit comes from what you pay them to produce your book, and they have no interest in whether you actually sell any copies.

There are many tasks that a bona fide publisher will under-take automatically, such as registering the ISBN number of your book (this is the number by which books are recognised, and you will usually find it just above the bar code) and distribution – i.e. getting your book into bookshops and to a wide audience. Some vanity publishers may suggest that they will undertake all the normal publisher's tasks, and that they are only asking you to contribute to the publication costs, but in reality the author is generally paying the entire bill. More often than not you are left with something that is not saleable and has cost you far too much. There are other ways to go if you are determined to see your work in print – such as self-publishing or Print on Demand.

Self-publishing and Print on Demand

If you feel that you are never going to make it with a mainstream publisher but desperately want your story in book form, there are some Print on Demand companies who will give you an estimate of what it will cost to produce bound copies. That way at least you know what you are paying for and how much you will have to do yourself. If you just want some copies for yourself and family, POD may be the best route – unless it's for a picture book, where printing costs can be exorbitant.

If you think you might be interested in self-publishing or in one of the many Print-on-Demand companies, read up on it first so that you are aware of the amount of effort and hard work this will entail on your part – not only in terms of layout and design, but also distribution and publicity.

There are books which have been self-published and then taken on by a mainstream publisher afterwards, but these are the exception. Self-publishing is not a route I would recommend for a first-time author unless you have a huge amount of time and energy to expend. There are many pitfalls for the inexperienced, so don't undertake it unless you have taken quite a bit of time to discover exactly what is required and how to get the most of all that money and effort you will expend in the process.

Unless you are particularly keen to get involved in all the different processes that a publisher employs skilled people to undertake, such as publicity and marketing, layout and design, copy-editing and so on, I would steer clear of this and concentrate on writing. If your work is good enough, a publisher will take it on, but it will take time and the main things you need are patience, perseverance and a willingness to take criticism and learn from it.

> If two or three people are saying the same negative thing about a piece of work, they are most likely right ... you need to try and take it on board and think it over. Praise does not improve your writing, but good, constructive criticism does.
>
> Rebecca Lisle

Rejection – and how to deal with it

Rejection is something that you need to brace yourself for, and it's not easy for anyone. No matter how successful you are or have been, rejection still happens and still hurts. You will hear tales of how many times a very successful book was rejected by agents and publishers and then went on to sell millions: agents and publishers will admit that they have no crystal ball and they make mistakes just like anyone else. It's all part of the process, and the sooner you try to accept that it's not personal, the better. *You* are not being rejected.

There will be reasons why an agent or publisher will reject your work which have no bearing on you personally – and at times no bearing on the quality of your writing, either. To succeed, you need: a tough skin; determination coupled with a good dollop of common sense; belief in yourself and your writing and enough modesty to realise when you might need help.

If you send your work out to a publisher you might get a standard rejection letter – i.e. many thanks, but …

- it's not for us
- it will not fit with our list
- we are not accepting unsolicited submissions

All of these are perfectly reasonable reasons for refusing your story, but if someone takes the trouble to mention something that might be of help to you, remember that they did not need to comment on your work. They have taken the time to do so out of a busy schedule, so the least you can do is acknowledge this and take their comments on board.

They may suggest that you look more carefully at where you are sending your work, which usually means that you have not really done your homework; alternatively they may explain that they are no longer accepting this kind of submission. This could be because their policy has changed and they are not looking for this kind of thing any more.

One story I had written got a very positive response from a senior editor, who then took it to a commissioning meeting.

Later she came back and told me that although she had loved my work, they had to reject it because they already had two or three books on that subject on their list. Did I have anything else? I was so depressed by this rejection that I threw it into a drawer where it languished for six months or more before I sent it out to another publisher on the recommendation of a writer friend. It was accepted for publication within a few weeks. What I should have done was to get another story ready and send it out to the keen editor immediately. It is all part of the learning process.

> We should consider what sort of book *we* want to write. If it's all castles in the air, then it might as well have the turrets and drawbridge chosen by us. **Celia Rees**

Don't assume that you are right and everyone else is wrong about your manuscript, but at the same time you have to believe in it enough to send it out again and again. This sounds like a contradiction, but there is a difference between arrogance and self-belief. You can believe in your work while still listening to suggestions and being prepared to learn. Accepting good advice may help to make your work the best it can be – and the most commercial.

There are a few items of basic common sense to bear in mind. You cannot expect a publisher to publish your story if you write:

- A story that is too old for the age range, in terms of complexity or subject matter.
- A story that responsible adults would think is unacceptable for the children it's aimed at.
- A story that is too long/short for their imprint.

The publisher's job is to sell books, not to print stories that will be rejected by children, parents or teachers, or books that don't fit in with their 'brand' or house style. Although there are always books that create a bit of a scandal because of their content, they are usually aimed at an older age, i.e. teenage readers who are more able to discern what is reasonable behaviour and are old enough to question what they read.

Rejection is hard to take, but it is a necessary evil. Whatever you do, don't take your manuscript to the publisher or agent in person and insist that you speak to them about it. It is the words that must sell your story, not you in person. One agent I know had someone turn up at her door, manuscript in hand. This is pointless and unlikely to make an agent look favourably at your work; in fact it will probably do the exact opposite. Nor should you ever call up and pester someone who has rejected your manuscript – it's not going to make them change their mind about your story, but it's likely to make them run a mile if they hear or see your name again. Not a good way to start out in publishing.

Their reasons for rejecting your work may not be obvious to you: no publisher or agent wants to reject something that may turn out to be the next bestseller, but they do have the experience to tell if something is not right. They may feel that the writing or the story/plot construction is not quite strong enough, or it may not be the kind of thing they feel is right for them to publish.

> Humility is the name of the game. If someone in the profession gives you advice, take it. If an editor tells you they liked your story but it wasn't quite right for them, don't assume everyone is out to get you. Take it on the chin, develop a thick skin and be prepared to LEARN, all the time, from everyone.
>
> **Joanna Kenrick**

Sometimes your story is just not something that appeals to a particular publisher or agent. That doesn't mean it will not appeal to someone else. A lot rests on personal choice, as well as experience of the market and, to some degree, instinct. In the end, if they say it's not for them, you have to accept the decision and move on.

Checklist and general summary

- Spend as much time as you can in the children's department of a good bookshop and **read everything you can**. Look for the copyright sign inside the book, to find titles that have been written within the last 3–4 years; in this way you can get an idea of structure, length, subject matter and approach. Get to know who publishes what in the age range you are keen to write for.

- Be **original**. Even a well known story or idea can be successful if handled in a fresh new way, or seen from a different perspective

- Be **professional**! This is not a game or a hobby for a busy publisher, editor or agent.

- Look for information on publishers and agents, and do thorough research on where to send your work. **Target** your work – don't use a scattergun approach!

- Always check to see **what a publisher or agent wants you to send,** either by email/letter enquiry or by checking their website.

- **Present your work** typed on one side of A4 paper, double spaced and numbered. Remember to include all your contact details on a cover sheet – with the title of your book – and indicate the number of words and the age/level it's aimed at. Include postage if you want it returned.

- With a picture book or short book, send the complete text. With a novel it's often better to send the **first three chapters and a synopsis**. Make sure that you have already completed the book before sending any of it out.

- Expect to get rejections and don't take it personally – use any suggestions to help you write better or to target your writing more specifically to the market. **Keep trying!**

Accepted for publication – what happens next

Congratulations! You have had a manuscript accepted for publication. It's the most wonderful feeling when someone sends you a letter or email, or perhaps calls you up to tell you that your manuscript has been accepted. Although you may be floating on a cloud of delight, be sure to act in a businesslike manner in all of your dealings with the company.

The editor may want to discuss illustrators, if it's a picture book, or they may want to talk about publication dates or request some re-writes. There will also be contractual issues to finalise: more information on this is covered in Section 4. But for the moment, enjoy and celebrate your success. It takes perseverance, talent and not a little luck to get this far. There are still many pitfalls ahead, and it's by no means certain that because you have one book published you now have a fully fledged writing career. So don't give up the day job – quite yet!

Section 4
Now You Are Published

22.

Fact Versus Fiction

Your dream has come true. You have made it over the first major hurdle – your manuscript has been accepted and you are looking forward to the day when you can finally show your brand new published book to the world.

You see yourself being invited to publishing parties; on the radio and television; as the darling of the press. Everyone knows your name and you are a celebrity. People stop you in the street and queue up to get your autograph. You can't wait for the applause and for all the cash to flow in!

That was fun – now for the reality. The unfortunate truth is that very little of this is likely to happen at all. Even if some of it does, it's not likely to be for quite a while. Nothing in publishing tends to happen quickly or as you would expect, your job is to find out as much as you can about how the system works and see what you can do to make sure that your book is not forgotten even before its life has properly begun.

You have been offered a contract and perhaps have discussed some things with your editor or agent, such as publication date, suggested advance and royalties (or one-off fee), and even foreign rights. Unless you know about these things, it is best not to agree to anything until you have taken advice. (For more information, *see* Chapter 28.)

The sad truth is that despite the eager interest you may have had from your editor/publishing company, your book may actually appear with less of a bang than a whimper – or even with complete silence. If you are lucky you may get an acknowledging card or perhaps even a bunch of flowers from your publisher on publication day, but don't hold your breath.

A few years ago it was suggested that I speak at the Edinburgh International Book Festival about having a career as a children's writer. This made me stop and think, because I had never really thought of my writing as a career – it was more something that had evolved, at times a little unexpectedly. So I looked up 'career' in the dictionary and it said:

> CAREER: *Swift course ... progress through life ... way of making a livelihood and advancing oneself ... to go swiftly or wildly.*
>
> **The Oxford Concise Dictionary**

The editor of that particular volume had possibly never tried to become a children's writer! The course is usually not particularly swift, although it can be a bit wild at times. Progress through life? We all do that anyway, but this is a career in which the progress is often slow and sometimes reversed, with the occasional leaps and bounds forward. These usually come just when you had given up all hope – part of the rollercoaster of emotions that are all part and parcel of being a writer.

When I asked one successful children's writer if she thought her career was what she had expected, she said, 'I don't think I ever thought about what it would be like, because I never thought I would get there; in fact I'm not sure I am.' How would she know? There is no designated career path, no structure or way of progressing that you can reliably expect to follow. With that in mind I decided that I should canvass the thoughts of some other children's writers. I asked them, 'Is being a children's writer anything like you had expected?'

> ... I never thought about it, beyond imagining what it would be like to be clutching my very own published book!
>
> **Julie Bertagna**

> Honestly I didn't think I'd be spending so much time away from my desk.
>
> **Catherine MacPhail**

So what does it mean to be a children's writer?

Writing for children is different from writing for adults, in that you are less likely to be 'pigeon-holed'. Publishers, booksellers and the reading public tend to recognise a writer by the genre they write in, so when you pick up a book by Stephen King or Ian Rankin you will generally know what kind of story to expect. As a writer of children's books, though, you may find that having published a children's novel or a picture book, you are at some point asked to write something for a different age group or in a completely different genre.

> As someone who started out as an illustrator, children's picture books seemed the obvious place to go for work that allowed plenty of fun and fantasy. Progressing into writing fiction for older children became a natural extension of that; a means of exploring ideas more complex and ambitious than I could achieve within the confines of the picture book.
>
> **Fiona Dunbar**

Many who seem to have achieved instant success as a children's writer have actually taken quite a long route to get there. That route is paved with persistence and hard graft, but it is different for everyone. Possibly this is the reason why most writers are asked, 'How did you get published?' Many writers have known since childhood that they wanted to write, while others may not have had this driving goal – there is no right or wrong way. Whatever has led you to be published has worked for you, and the trick is to keep going, be open to opportunities, and be realistic about the market.

It can often take four or five years from actually signing your first contract to being able to write full-time, and it may never happen at all or to any particular timescale.

23.

Writing Full-time

Interestingly, I asked a few non-writers what they thought a children's writer did all day. My neighbour said, 'Sitting at your computer thinking up ideas and writing most of the time.' A friend said, 'You probably spend time with your kids, your household chores, walking the dog, etc. Can't take long to write a children's book, especially one with very few words!! Probably time spent imagining, putting your mind in a child's world, making coffee and talking to your friends. Not got a clue,' she finally admitted, 'but it's not a full-time job – you couldn't write all day. Perhaps some time each week; then you would do other things.'

In some ways my friend was right, because a writer doesn't spend all day physically writing. Often it seems like all the other things connected with writing threaten to take up so much of your time that you have to be very disciplined to make sure you leave time to write!

Every day is different, and every writer is different. Here are some of the things that might take up your time:

- **Writing at the computer**. That's my particular preference, but some prefer to write by hand. Re-writing, printing it out, reading it again. Work always reads better from paper, for some reason.
- **Fixing the printer/computer** which has decided to go on the blink just as you are desperate to print out the pages of your newly finished novel, or you have just pressed the wrong button and lost the whole morning's work.
- **Research for new book**. This can involve a lot of time, or a little. It can involve travel, visits to museums and libraries to speak to experts. It can even involve learning a new skill.

- **Answering letters/fan mail.**
- **Meetings and outings.** These include meetings with publishers, agents, the writing community, and related organisations. Events and meetings are also good opportunities to meet up with other writers and people in the publishing industry.
- **Preparing for events/workshops.** Perhaps these are tailored to the latest book.
- **Time spent organising author visits.** See under Section 4, on school and library visits. A lot of organisation is required before any visit.
- **Travelling to schools or other visit venues.**
- **Answering the phone and making calls, writing and sorting though emails, sending and chasing invoices.** All of this can be incredibly time-consuming and can destroy your train of thought or the emotional calm needed for writing. At other times it can be a displacement activity.

You cannot possibly write all the time or concentrate for hours on end without some time to drift, and writers find that this 'drifting' time can be incredibly creative. The problem is that it can be difficult to know when it is productive and when it becomes an excuse to avoid the next bit of writing.

> Switch off your email while at the computer. The Internet and email are tyrants and very bad for you. But we love and need them. Balancing that is the key. **Nicola Morgan**

Some people said that the **worst things** about being a children's writer were:

- All the other things you do that take you away from actually writing.
- The fact that it can be quite lonely at times, working away in your own head.
- Demands thrown at you by publishers that take you away from your desk. Then in the same breath they ask when the next book will be ready.
- Far too much paperwork (letters from schools, libraries, emails, tax accounts, royalties).

126

- Foreign rights and contracts that seem impossible to understand.
- Working for peanuts.
- Going into bookshops and *not* finding your book there.

But quoted as being the **best things** about being a children's writer were:

- Being paid to daydream and follow your imagination.
- Being able to do it anywhere, anytime – not tied to the 9–5 daily grind.
- Being able to be flexible – working around family commitments, etc.
- Going into schools and speaking to your readers; finding out what they think and what they like to read.

> I like writing for children because they are the audience most willing to suspend disbelief and really share a story with an author.   **Pippa Goodhart**

Finally there is the constant drive as a writer to write an even better book next time. Even if you never got paid for it, you know you would just have to keep on doing it. We do it because we love it.

> If my doctor told me I had only six minutes to live, I wouldn't brood. I'd type a little faster.   **Isaac Asimov**

The writing community

Writing can seem quite a lonely process at times. You sit at your desk writing away and sometimes wonder if anyone really understands what it's like: the highs and lows, the frustrations and the joys. Chances are that your family and friends are delighted that you are a published writer but have no real understanding of what to expect or what you are experiencing.

Often they get just as excited as you about possible future

successes and even more disappointed (is that possible?) when something is rejected. This isn't especially helpful and the best solution is to speak to other writers who know exactly how you feel. There are associations you may want to join, such as the Scattered Authors Society (*see* page 171), which comprises published children's authors 'scattered' (as the name suggests) across the length and breadth of the UK. The Society of Authors holds meetings and social events where you can meet other authors, as well as regional meetings and sub-groups for Children's Writers and Illustrators (CWIG) and Educational Writers and Illustrators (EWIG). The Society of Children's Writers and Book Illustrators (SCWBI), is an international organisation with regional divisions for both published and unpublished writers.

The launch party

Unless your publisher is organising a launch party, which is unlikely unless they have paid a fortune for your book, you might do better to organise one yourself. This might sound a little depressing, but if you write a children's book looking for fame and fortune you are likely to be disappointed. Most writers write because they desperately want to, not because of promised rewards – delightful though these might be when they do come along.

The fact is that there are many books published every year and yours is only one of them, so unless there is a particular reason for your work to stand out from the crowd it might just disappear. There is advice in Chapter 25 to help you avoid this, and another way to ensure that your precious story gets some publicity is a launch party.

Your editor will have moved on to other books long before yours reaches its publication date, and it's unlikely that they will have much (or any) publicity budget to back your book. It does seem quite ridiculous that any commercial enterprise would put themselves to a lot of expense to publish a book and then be prepared to let it languish unnoticed on the shelves – but unfortunately it does seem to happen.

What your publisher may agree to is a contribution towards the cost of your launch event. Perhaps enough to cover the wine? When deciding where to host your party, you may want to choose an unusual venue or enlist a local school or group to help; this might encourage press interest too. Contact your local library or bookshop and see if they might be happy to organise a launch: this will save you the expense of hiring a venue, and if you or your publisher pay for the wine, the bookshop will handle the stock and the sale of your books. This leaves you free to chat to your guests, make a very short welcome speech, and perhaps read a bit of your book before signing any copies your guests might like to buy.

You will probably find that unless you have a lot of friends who are writers, most of your family and friends will never have been to a book launch before and will be delighted to be invited – especially with 'first edition signed copies' available to buy. To a lot of people, as soon as you have a published book you are a celebrity of sorts and they will bask in the glory of announcing to others that they are the personal friend of a published author. They want you to be successful so that they can share the reflected glory. So why not make it an excuse to throw a party and enjoy yourself? You have earned it.

Would you read my manuscript?

Once you are published you may be asked by unpublished writers to read and comment on their work. Having been in their position, we can all recognise the way they feel and want to be helpful. Unfortunately this can be a slippery slope: they tend to hope that a published writer will be able to show them the magic route to instant publication, and possibly fame and fortune!

Be a little cautious and think about it before agreeing. Aside from the fact that reading and commenting on someone else's work will take up some of your own precious writing time and energy, there may be all sorts of hidden expectations within a request of this nature. Make sure it is not a 'no win' situation for you.

Although it is lovely to be asked for your 'expert' opinion, I have heard of writers who have lost friends of long standing because they read a piece of their work and told them the truth: that it was less than perfect. If you take the time to read someone's writing and you think it is terrible, how would you tell them? We all know how difficult it is to take criticism and, despite their assurances, people often do not want to hear that you think their precious story is not 'wonderful'.

One way around this could be agreeing to read a couple of chapters only, which is what an editor would do. Make it clear that you can only offer them an opinion – and that the only opinion that really matters in publishing is that of the person who agrees to publish it. That is not you.

A note on bookshops

Given the number of new books published every month, book-shops can never stock them all (and that doesn't take into account all the other books that have been published in past years and those classics they will always stock). So your book will have a lot of competition. It is worth spending some of your precious time getting to know your local bookshop. Offer to come in and sign some books or do events – but make sure you look at Chapter 25 of this book on self-promotion, and the subsequent chapter on school visits and other events, to make sure that you make the best use of your time and energies.

24.

What to Expect of Your Publisher/Agent

To you, your book is the most important one ever to be published. To your publisher, agent and bookseller it is just one among many. So be realistic in your expectations, and undertake as much as you can to promote your own work. For more advice on this, *see* Chapter 25.

Your publisher

> I've always found that if I expect nothing, then it makes me feel special whenever they do something visibly helpful.
>
> **Mark Robson**

When your book is finally finished and accepted for publication, it will go through various stages, as set out below.

You have laboured over the manuscript and your publisher wants to publish it – so you may think that it's all up to them from here on. But why would you work so hard on your book just to hand it over to someone else and do nothing more? You can and should remain actively involved in the publishing process; after all, this is your 'baby'!

The editing process

Your publisher will assign an editor to your project. He or she should be the one with the critical eye who will go through the manuscript to root out any problems or inconsistencies. The amount of editing will depend on various things, but generally your editor will suggest any changes he or she thinks might enhance the finished book – perhaps some alterations to plot or character to bring out emotion or pace.

It could be that some of this has been worked up before the book was accepted, so that the editor has only minor suggestions. The best relationship between writer and editor is one of trust, where the writer trusts that the editor understands their book.

The following is an extract from an article in *Armadillo*, by Mary Hoffman.

Fliers and Catchers: Author, Gillian Cross; Editor, Liz Cross – On writing and editing. Without conferring, each described what authors want from editors, and vice versa.

How editors would like authors to be
(As imagined by author Gillian Cross)
- a fount of up-to-the-minute ideas
- open to discussing all possibilities and pitfalls of the idea before writing anything
- a really good team player
- someone who writes for recognisable niches
- personally memorable, flamboyant and eccentric

How editors actually want authors to be
(As described by editor Liz Cross)
- VERY patient (all editors are dominated by guilt)
- able to nag 'nicely'
- good at meeting deadlines
- open to editing
- having a clear vision for their own work
- recognising boundaries
- having a rare and precious talent

How authors want editors to be
(Gillian Cross's personal list)
- able to see the potential of the 'pitched' idea
- willing to take the risk

- able to ask open-ended and perceptive questions, NOT suggestions
- prepared to give a contract and a deadline
- willing to 'go away for a long time'
- responsive to delivered text within two or three weeks at most
- enthusiastic
- able to put their finger on anything wrong
- confidence-building
- respectful that it is the author's book
- consultative about changes
- able to write the blurb better than the author

How authors would like editors to be
(as perceived by Liz Cross)
- prompt and communicative
- honest
- the author's friend (in terms of making the book what the author intended)
- a representative of the author within the publishing house
- a midwife
- a 'catcher to the trapeze-artist's flier of the author' (using Alan Garner's metaphor)

Copy-editing and proofreading

As well as a commissioning/managing editor, a little further down the line your book will be assigned to a copy-editor – someone with a fresh eye who checks the manuscript for structure, spelling and other errors, and general inconsistencies.

This is your last chance to go over your work and check that you are happy with it. Once it is passed to the typesetters, anything other than minor changes start to cost money. Everything should be checked substantially before this stage is reached.

Once the typesetter has set the layout, first proof copies are sent out both to the author and to a professional proofreader (who may or may not be the same person as the copy-editor). In the main, at this point you should only be checking for any errors introduced in the typesetting process. Hopefully at the same time the editor begins to send out some proof copies to obtain good quotes for the cover, and to make people aware of its impending publication.

The cover of your book

Some publishers will put books that they feel are particularly suitable for either girls or boys in covers to match. So books about princesses and fairies, all pink and fluffy, are often good sellers for girls, while boys' books tend to have comic illustrations or action covers. This doesn't mean that girls won't read them; just that this is the way in which they will be marketed. Boys are likely to be drawn to non-fiction and action books – but many girls like these, too.

The cover of your book is an incredibly important sales tool because it is the first thing a prospective buyer will see. It must have impact and carry the right message about what is inside the book. While your publisher is experienced in the market and – hopefully – has the input of a team of expert marketing and sales people, you may at some time or other have mixed feelings about the cover chosen for your book.

While you might expect to have some say in this important decision, in fact the final say about the cover does lie with your publisher. Having said that, while recognising the expertise of those who are producing your book you are entitled to your opinion … so if you feel very strongly that the cover should be changed, then say so. Publishers do sometimes get things wrong. If you have good reason to object to the cover – and after all, who knows your book better than you? – prepare a good, balanced argument and you may succeed in having your way. However, you should also accept that you may be outvoted. Your book has taken long hours of heartfelt toil to produce, and it is possible that you are simply too 'close' to it.

I have had covers that I particularly liked, one of which was an educational book entitled *The Grey Boatman*. Published in the USA it had a mysterious and enticing cover, but when the same title came out in Australia it had a different one – partly because it was teamed up with another story in an anthology so that the cover was split in half. Both stories featured cartoon sketches on the cover, giving the reader no clue as to the type of story that lay within.

I know of one author who had written an edgy novel for boys that girls would also like to read. However, the designer had not read the whole book and the cover was not one that a boy of that age could easily carry without being teased. Another author said she had had some covers that she loved, but which also featured some huge mistakes – such as the one where the main character was of the wrong sex, and others that contained errors in the blurb.

Some books have great covers that make you want to discover the story inside. This is how it should be. My favourite covers include Vivian French's *Robe of Skulls*, Debi Gliori's *Goodnight Baby Bat!*, and David Almond's *Skellig*. Bear in mind that these all feature great stories. No matter how good a cover is, it will never make a bad book good.

Publicity

Your publisher's publicity and marketing people should hopefully get in touch with you sometime between signing the contract and delivery of the manuscript. They might send you an author's publicity form to fill in, which tells them about you and anything they might be able to use to promote you and your book.

The reality is that children's books do not often get reviewed in newspapers unless the publisher has paid an extraordinarily large advance for it. If there is anything quirky or especially interesting about an author, this can increase their chances of getting noticed by the media. One publicist from a major publisher told me: 'If a new author has an interesting back-story – for example, something they did before becoming an author, or a weird or interesting hobby – it can help get them a mention in the national papers.'

If you do, and are willing to give interviews, the publicist may be able to get you a review in a hobby magazine, a slot on local radio, or a feature in the papers. If you are keen to talk to the media, make sure that you don't just jump in – your publisher may be on the verge of submitting a carefully prepared and timed news item. Communication is particularly important here.

You can ask your publisher's publicity team what they are doing to promote your book, and then think about what you can do or suggest to them that will go along with it or add to their plans. Helpful suggestions and ideas can be passed on, but try to make sure you are being realistic; cost is always a major factor in any publicity budget, and some books simply have no publicity budget at all. This is where creative ideas that don't cost the publisher anything are welcomed.

Writing a successful series can be very profitable for both writer and publisher – often much more so than one-off titles. The publisher finds it easier to promote a series, and children and parents recognise it. Often they will look for a series more readily than for single books. In marketing speak this is because they are a 'brand', although some authors such as Jacqueline Wilson and Anne Fine have become famous for their particular style of writing, which is immediately recognisable, even if they are not writing series books.

Don't expect to go on a book tour across the country unless you are a top author with a string of bestsellers behind you. You *can* expect your publisher to produce your book at the allotted time, and to have copies ready for the launch date. If you are planning your own launch party (*see* pp. 128–129), check that the books will be available in time – or, better still, well in advance.

Your agent

You don't have to have an agent; some writers prefer not to, instead handling all negotiations and the business side of writing themselves. If you feel secure enough in your knowledge of the publishing world, you may not want or need an agent.

If you are a novice, wanting to expand your writing into different areas, or just feel that you want someone to fight your corner, then you may decide to look for an agent. Publishers are happy to consider submissions from reputable agents, because they know that if a book comes to them via this route it has already been through one level of 'filtering'. Many publishers no longer have readers in-house, so agents are often the first to read a manuscript.

If you have an agent, then, it means your manuscript is more likely to be read – and read reasonably quickly, than if it is an unsolicited submission. Even when publishers are not accepting unsolicited manuscripts, they will usually look at something that comes in from an agent.

What do agents look for in a writer?

An agent makes their income from clients who are published, or who are likely to become published. If their client's book does not get published, they will earn nothing. The usual practice is for them to deduct 10–15% from any advances, royalties or other payments the book earns, as per your contract with them. An agent may be willing to take on an unpublished writer whose book is almost ready for publication but perhaps needs some editing: some agents will do more editorial work than others.

When you are offered a contract with a publisher, your agent will vet it and try to get you the best terms they can. They will be looking after your interests and will try to get the publisher to change or delete clauses in the contract that may not be in your favour. Contracts are, by their very nature, full of legal jargon, and this is where your agent is a great help; they should be able to explain any clause that you find confusing. Always read your contract carefully, and ask your agent to explain anything that you don't understand.

What to look for in an agent

Your agent should be able to advise you what publishers are currently looking for, and if your ideas for future books are likely to appeal and are commercial. However, don't expect them to have a crystal ball. They will be able to obtain publishers' briefs for any particular series you may want to write for; once you have written your book they will send it out to publishers they know are in the market for that kind of book.

An agent with good contacts will be having ongoing conversations with publishers and might suggest that they have something that the publisher would be interested in: your book. They may take your book to the book fairs in London, Bologna or Frankfurt to show to publishers or foreign buyers there. If you are an established writer in a particular age group or genre, your agent may be able to secure a contract on some chapters and a synopsis.

How to get an agent

Ideally you should try to meet your agent so you know that you can work together and develop a good business relationship.

Before you apply to an agency, do some investigative work. Find out which companies have an agent who will deal with children's books – not all do. You should consider whether you want an agent who works for themselves or in a small agency with just one or two partners, or if you would be happier approaching a large literary agency.

When you contact your chosen agency, take time to find out the relevant agent's name. Look at their website to see what kind of submissions they prefer, so that you get started on the right foot, then send a letter or email addressed to them personally. Much of the advice in Section 3 on submitting to a publisher is relevant to applying to an agency: most of all, do your research and be professional.

Although the choice is yours as to whom to approach, there is no guarantee that the agent you want will be prepared to take you on as a client, even if you have a record of publication. When looking for new clients, agents want writers who are likely to have a writing career ahead of them – not someone who just wants to write one book, or write for fun. They want writers who are serious about their writing and, if not yet published, who in their opinion have the potential to be published.

It used to be the case that multiple submissions to agents (i.e. sending your manuscript to different agencies at the same time) were not appreciated, but these days it is deemed acceptable as long as you let them know what you are doing. If you are successful in securing an agent, you must inform the other agencies you approached as soon as possible, so that they don't waste their time.

Getting the right agent is important. You have to feel able to discuss your ideas, hopes and even your fears with them. You have to value their judgement, even if you do not always agree with everything they say, and you need to feel sure that they are working for you. Occasionally writers feel that their agent isn't proactive enough on their behalf. By all means keep in regular contact with your agent, and enquire as to their progress – but bear in mind that they are very busy. They want your book to do well: that is their livelihood. Your part of the contract is to act in a reasonable manner, remembering that you are not their only client and, if your book is not yet earning them much of an income, they still have to earn a crust. If an agent has taken you on, it's your responsibility to treat your writing seriously and not to expect them to spend time on your manuscript when you are not prepared to do the same.

It can be as difficult to find a good agent as it is to find a publisher for your book. If you don't have an agent but need advice, you can always have your publishing contract vetted by the Society of Authors by becoming an associate member, if you have not been published before. They will not negotiate on your behalf, but are happy to discuss your contract in detail with you. Their legal department will explain clauses that you do not understand, advising you which ones to query with your publisher.

25.

Self-promotion

It's all too easy to feel that the world owes you a stage for having contributed to literature by writing a book, but take a look around – there are thousands of others in the same position, all wanting to promote their work ahead of you. For some lucky few, the publishers will decide to throw their marketing weight behind a book. If that's you, congratulations! Sit back and enjoy the ride.

For the rest ... well, it's time to roll up your sleeves and show the world what you can do without Richard and Judy's help.

Mark Robson

Just because you can write a book that is good enough to get published doesn't mean that you like being in the public eye. Standing up addressing a room full of strangers or speaking on radio or television is some people's idea of a nightmare.

Unfortunately these days the culture of celebrity means that your publisher will not only look at the wonderful book you have written, but if the book is successful they will also want you to be there promoting it in lots of different ways. There are writers who love this and are very good at it; others make a virtue of being invisible, using that to create a mystique about themselves.

Writers who are successful at self-promotion do it in different ways and a lot depends on your own personality. Some are wonderfully charming to everyone, remember names and generally smooze their way into the public eye. Others get there through sheer perseverance and are always willing to speak generally pushing themselves forward at any opportunity.

At the extremes, both of these can be irritating, but these methods used sensibly do appear to work in terms of getting yourself known. Some children's authors do incredible amounts of school visits. This takes a huge amount of time and energy but it does spread the word about your books. You have to be very disciplined to make sure you have time to continue writing and don't lose sight of the fact that the only reason you have something to publicise is because you have written the book in the first place. It does become a little easier the more you do.

> The more you can do, the better – but never do more than you are comfortable with. Stay true to yourself and don't let anyone make you feel guilty about what you do or don't do. Writing is more important than promoting.   **Nicola Morgan**

It's a good idea to put together some kind of a plan of the things you can do to promote your books. Even if you don't do all of them all the time, you can keep the plan pinned to your wall and plug away at it whenever you can. Here are some areas you may want to think about, and some ideas to get you started.

Your publisher

Get to know the publicity people in your publishing house, and also the sales force. These are the ones who will be promoting your book, so without being a pest get to know who they are and offer to help or suggest ideas. They will be working to a budget (unfortunately, sometimes no budget at all for your book), so make sure your ideas are practical and not ridiculously extravagant.

Ask if they might produce some bookmarks, posters or postcards of the cover of your book. You can also use these as invitations if you are having a book launch (*see* pp. 128–129). You can get them printed yourself if the publisher is not keen to do it, and they might contribute to the costs. At the very least ask, you have nothing to lose. If you have a website, ask them to put your website address on the bookmarks or postcards.

Branding

Much as you might hate the idea, think of yourself as a brand. What is your USP (Unique Selling Point)? What makes you and your book different from all the others? What is there about you that might interest the newspapers? They are always looking for an angle, something quirky or different.

One of the difficulties that children's writers find with this idea is that they can be several different 'brands'. If you write picture books, that is one audience; older books might be another. If you also write teenage books you will be in an entirely different market. This doesn't need to be a problem but you do need to recognise what the different areas require so that you are prepared to market yourself in different ways.

You can ask to see your sales figures and find out where your books do best so that you can target any weaker areas. If they are doing a press release, ask to see this too. Be pleasant and polite, remembering that you are asking them to take time to deal with your request, so being friendly can only help your chances of a good response.

Bookshops

Bookshops are always keen to get authors in to sign books. Get to know your local independent bookshop: they are often incredibly enthusiastic and helpful when it comes to promoting a local author. In the bigger book chains, make yourself known to the children's booksellers and chat to the children's buyer if you can. Offer to come in and do an event. As a rule you get paid for events in schools and libraries, etc. but not for going into bookshops. If you can, get to know the influential people who buy for the larger chain bookshops and make sure that they know about your book.

AI (Author Information) sheet

Make sure you get a good publicity photo. Have it ready to send/email out along with a short and interesting biography and a list of any books you have published.

If your publisher is not preparing one, you might want to put together an Author Information (AI) sheet. This would feature your publicity photo, some blurb/biography about you – and perhaps the cover of your new/latest book with a short blurb and quotes from any good reviews. Don't forget to have the publisher's information on it, the ISBN number and your website address.

Try to think of some interesting things about yourself; past jobs or quirky experiences that might add to your interest. Look at other author's websites and publicity information to see examples. It can seem as though everyone else has had a more interesting life than you have, but you are a writer – you can make anything sound exciting, so why not your own experiences?

Librarians and teachers

Get to know your local Literacy Co-ordinator and let them know you are available for school and library visits (or perhaps offer to do workshops). Your local school librarian and the youth librarian of your area library service are good contacts to make. They have a wealth of information about what is going on in your area in the libraries and schools, and again let them know you are available for workshops or school/library visits. If you are planning a visit to a different area, find out the name of the youth librarian or Literacy Co-ordinator for that area and see if they can help to organise something there.

Agent

Make sure your agent is working for you: ask if they are putting your name forward. Agents get requests for authors for different events and projects, but it's not always practical for them to keep telling you whenever they do this because nothing may come of it. If you ask, they should be able to tell you about anything that has come in recently and this might remind them that you are keen to be put forward.

Events

If you are doing an event, make sure that it's being promoted. Put it up on your website (you may find people contacting you saying things like, 'I didn't know you would speak to that age group. Perhaps you could come and do something here with us?').

Check to see if the organiser of any events you are doing has contacted the local press, and get to know the local journalists who might cover a story. Drop them an email if you are doing something unusual or in their area.

Make sure that your books are available at such events. Take any publicity material you have with you, or if you have a poster, send it out well in advance.

The media

When promoting yourself and your book, don't underestimate the power of the media. Don't be shy about getting in touch with reporters; look for an angle they can use to run a story about you or your book. Even the local paper running a story might lead to one of the nationals taking it up, if they think they can make something out of it.

Don't forget to use the press or your local radio or TV station, and keep an eye on topical news stories and to see if anything you are doing might tie in with the latest news or political announcement. Have short quotes ready – and offer them. Get your name out there and keep it actively in the public eye.

Networking

Get to know people. Join societies and organisations and get to know the writers, agents, publishers, booksellers and librarians in your area. Once you get your name on various lists you will find invitations follow to book launches, exhibition openings and all sorts of other networking opportunities.

When you are there, don't hog the wall. Step forward and speak to people, be pleasant and friendly and listen. It's amazing the information you can pick up. Everyone knows what it's like to be the new person on the block, and one thing I can say for children's writers is that they are generally a friendly and welcoming bunch, who are very willing to be helpful to newcomers.

The only word of caution is that if you are naturally gregarious and extrovert there is a slight danger of being overly friendly and pushy. People will remember you better and be more inclined to invite you to other events and into their company if you have a good attitude. You will not endear yourself to anyone if you come over as the arrogant newcomer. Often the quietest person standing beside you might be the most experienced and established author.

> Be humble without being timid; be forthright without being arrogant; be positive without being pushy. In short – be nice!
>
> **Mark Robson**

Don't forget to use the Internet as a promotional tool, depending on how comfortable you are with this kind of thing and how much time you are prepared to put towards it. If you are so inclined you might write a blog or perhaps put up a download of you speaking or reading one of your books, on your website.

Everywhere you can promote yourself will add to your presence and the public perception that you are successful. The unfortunate truth of our society is that people who are very good at publicity can become much more successful over those who don't, often regardless of their creative abilities. So make the most of your books and don't neglect publicity just because it seems too difficult or uncomfortable. The more you speak in public, radio or TV, the easier it all becomes.

Your website

Most authors have websites, and these vary widely. They may be technically wonderful or just plain and informative. You don't have to have an all-singing, all-dancing website, but it should always be easy to read, rich in accessible information, and interesting enough to make people want to come back again.

The cost of building a website can also vary tremendously, and if you are computer literate it may be something you want to try yourself. Alternatively you can get someone to do it for you. Remember that your site is part of your visual appearance and it is important that it looks good and does what it is there for. Here are a few things to think about:

- *How much can you afford to spend?* Decide on your budget. Occasionally a publisher may be interested in helping you with your website, or even producing one for you, but the chances are you will have to fund it yourself (although this is an expense that can go against tax if you earn enough to pay tax on your writing earnings).
- *What do you want your website to do?* Do you want it to sell your books, to give your readers information about you and your books, or to give teachers and event organisers somewhere to find out what you can do and what you have written? What else do you want it to do? Do you want to entertain children with puzzles or quizzes?
- *Think about who you want to attract.* You need to consider this, and decide what you want to use your website for. Look at your target market. If you write predominantly for young children, your website has to be child-friendly, and will probably also be visited more often by adults or adults with their children than by children on their own. If you write for teenagers you may want a cool-looking website that will speak directly to them.

- *Think of yourself as a brand.* Try to think of yourself from the outside. What do you want people to see and what are you trying to promote?
- *Contact.* Make sure it is easy for people to contact you through your website, either via a form or by email, and get advice about avoiding spam. It is a good idea to set up a separate email address just for the website, so that if spam becomes a problem you can stop using it altogether and get a new one.
- *Blog.* Writing a blog or diary is one way to keep your site active and can be a way of getting people to revisit it to see what's new. You can also have a blog elsewhere and include a link to it on your site.
- *Details of books and selling opportunities.* You can use the site to sell your books; incorporate links to publishers and to online book sites such as Amazon.
- *About yourself.* Make this as interesting and different as you can and put in pictures or other images to make it fun. Look at other authors' websites to see how they have written about themselves. Remember that you should only put up on the Internet as much information as you are happy to share with the world; you may not want your address or telephone number on it. Some authors have only their agent's contact details (always check with them first); others only have email, which may be enough because anyone looking at your website obviously has access to the Internet and to email.
- *Links* – so that your website can be linked to others. Put interesting and relevant links on your website, but if you are wanting to attract children make sure anything you include is appropriate to their age. You can also feature links to other writers' sites – always ask if they will put a link to your site, too.
- *Events* you do (or can do) with details for event organisers. Your website is a good place to advertise any public events you have coming up, and also some of the interesting ones you may do – if possible with pictures. Again, be careful that you have parental permission to put any child's picture up on the web. Usually the safest thing is to try and get photos that are taken from behind the children. If there are pictures taken

for newspapers the schools will have already asked for this kind of permission from the parents, but always check and make sure.

Other considerations

Make sure that any writing on the site is easy to read, that there are no long blocks of text – people are not likely to read long pages, so feature lots of short pieces – and photographs, pictures or other interesting images to break up the text. Take a look at the websites of other authors to see what appeals to you, what is easy to read and how easy it is to find the information you want.

Try to get a website address that is not too complicated or difficult to remember. Many authors just use their own name.

Once you have a website, try to make sure that people know about it. Put it as a signature at the end of your outgoing emails; ask your publisher to add it to any promotional material like bookmarks and posters. Get some business cards printed, or print them yourself and make sure that your email and website addresses are on them.

Finally, always keep your website up to date. Sites that feature 'old' information give the user the impression that everything on them is no longer relevant.

26.

School and Other Author Events

You have to get good at the public side of things fairly quickly, as so much is expected of authors – particularly children's authors, who are also required to be entertaining. This is demanding and the opposite of sitting at your desk writing.

Julie Bertagna

As a published author you may be asked into schools and libraries, perhaps to speak at book festivals or conferences, and to sign books in bookshops or take part in all sorts of projects. How much of it do you need to do? Often a large part of a children's writer's income can come from author visits to schools and libraries, speaking at festivals, etc. The extent of your involvement really depends on you and sometimes on the kind of book you have written.

Author visits get your books and your name out into the population, while earning you some money to help with the cash flow after your advance is spent and until the time when you start to earn royalties or get an advance on a new book. They allow you to keep in touch with your readers and can provide inspiration for new writing.

When considering offers for author events, think about how far you are prepared to travel. How many children are you happy to speak to at once? What age of children are you comfortable with? What kind of thing would you want to do: would you rather talk about your books or about being an author, or run a reading or a workshop? How many sessions are you prepared to do in one day?

Schools and libraries

Visits to schools and libraries can be interesting and useful but at times you will encounter schools that are unprepared and disinterested, and staff that are impolite at best. Being well prepared beforehand can help to avoid bad experiences.

If you have been a teacher, you may feel that going into a school or library is less daunting than if you have never had to stand up and speak in public. But even if you have been a teacher, you are likely to be a little nervous here because your role is completely different.

Once again I will repeat something that comes up again and again: *be professional.* If you are being paid (and as an author going into a school or library, you should always be paid) you owe it to the organiser and the children to act in a professional manner. The best way is to start as you mean to go on from the first contact call or email. To enable you to do this you have to have thought about it beforehand.

Books for younger children often lend themselves to entertaining author events, and with a little bit of effort on your part (and perhaps some props) you can make your events exciting and fun for everyone concerned. Whatever the age of your audience, it is always a good idea to get the children to participate rather than have them as passive listeners. Try to involve them with questions and discussions around the theme of your book or your life as an author.

Usually an hour is plenty of time to be speaking to any one group. If the children are nursery age or very young, less time is often better to avoid them becoming tired and fidgety. Don't worry if very young children get a bit squirmy or glazed-looking when you are reading to them; this is fairly common and doesn't mean they aren't listening. Don't be put off by questions that seem completely out of context unless they are happening too often and halting the flow for the rest of the class.

Workshops may take longer – perhaps an hour and a half or two hours – and can involve a lot more preparation. Make sure you agree beforehand on how long you will be in contact with the children, and what kind of workshop the school is looking for.

Go and listen to other children's authors when they are visiting your local school/library or talking at a book festival. If you know any established children's authors, you might ask if they would mind if you came along to a school with them to observe. Most children's authors are very approachable and happy to help and advise.

At first you may not be asked into many schools, but this can quickly escalate so it's a good idea to keep re-evaluating how much time you are prepared to spend on school visits and away from actual writing.

Preparation

Sit down and look at your book to see what you can do with it. You know it better than anyone else; think about which elements are most important and if at all possible look for themes that might fit in with the curriculum. The teachers will love that and will tell their colleagues, which will result in more invitations. If you are not sure, ask a teacher for that age group and they may be able to help.

Think of props you might be able to make or buy to take with you. Picture books work well with cuddly toys, but try to come up with something unique to your book that will add interest. If you are an illustrator, the children will love it if you draw something for them.

Look at ways in which you can get the children to interact with you; this makes them feel part of the session. You might ask what kind of stories they like; invite them to guess how a story might end, and suggest an alternative ending; or discuss how one of your characters might solve a problem from your book in a different way.

It's a good idea to talk about how you write, where and how you started, and perhaps the different stages your book went through. Show them the proof of the cover if you have it, and ask them what they think. Tell them anecdotes about your life – when you were their age, at school, perhaps admitting to things you weren't good at then.

I like to bring children up to the front and give each of them a title of a job involved in bringing the book from my idea until it arrives in the bookshops. This gives them some idea of career possibilities, how many people are involved in publishing, and why authors don't get the full cover price of each book sold – a common misapprehension!

Be prepared for the usual questions and think about how you want to answer or avoid some of them. For example, How old are you? Where do you write? What is your favourite book? How much do you earn? Are you as rich as JK?

You will usually be invited to speak to children of the age at which your book is targeted, but this is not always the case, so check beforehand. Make sure that the classes suggested by the school are appropriate to your book and that you are happy speaking to children of that age. There is no point agreeing to speak to a nursery class if you feel unhappy with children younger than five years old.

Make sure the school doesn't try to get you to speak to more children than you are comfortable with. Teachers sometimes think they are getting better value by bringing more children into a session, but if you specify at the beginning that you are only happy to speak to one or perhaps two classes, they have no excuse to usher in the entire primary school. Some will still try to do it – so be warned.

Sometimes too wide an age group in a primary school can make it impossible for the visiting writer. You end up either targeting your talk to the youngest and boring the older ones, or making the little ones fidgety because it's all above them. It's often useful to point this out if it looks like teachers are keen to bring everyone in at once. They may seem to feel there is more value in numbers of children getting to meet an author than the quality of the experience for the child; I think it is just that they haven't thought about it, so politely point it out and all should be fine.

You also need to watch that the school doesn't suggest that you drop in and speak to yet another class, perhaps the little ones, while you are there. This is unfair as it never involves another fee and has not been agreed beforehand. It can be difficult to refuse but at times you have to be as barefaced as they are, and politely, but firmly, say no.

Trialling – you talk for free!

If you have not done any school visits before and are nervous about them, why not offer to go into your local school and suggest that you will do it for free. They are likely to be delighted, but don't agree to do too much or to unreasonable demands just because you don't like to say no. Remember that they are getting an author in for free, which they know would normally cost a full fee. This may sound harsh, but ask any author who regularly visits schools and you'll find that some or all of these things have happened to them. Most schools and teachers are wonderful and arrange events that make you delighted to go the extra mile.

Some writers will do a full or half day in a school; others will do no more than two or three sessions of about an hour each. It is not the same, despite what might be suggested, as the teacher talking to their own class for an hour; each session is a performance and the children are new to you and you to them. You are not there as a substitute teacher.

Fees for author visits

The Society of Authors suggests that the minimum fee, before expenses, should be £300 for a full day. In Scotland, if you are on Scottish Book Trust's Live Literature Funding database of writers, rates are currently £150 per session plus expenses (sessions are usually about one hour or as agreed beforehand). You are always free to charge what you want and some authors charge more and some less, but these are the suggested minimum, which you can quote to organisers. The fee is not merely to cover time spent in contact with the class and it is useful to consider – and point out if necessary – exactly what an author visit entails.

A school fee has to cover all the time spent travelling to and preparing for the visit, as well as all the time spent away from your desk not writing. It is not a good idea to make a habit of offering your services for free. This not only undervalues your efforts but it also sets a precedent in the school or teacher's mind. This is unreasonable; try asking a teacher or a plumber to work regularly for no pay.

A recent survey by the Society of Authors found that the average author earned less than £5000 per year from writing, and that for many children's authors school visits are a necessary part of their income. Teachers often seem surprised at the fee a writer might charge for visiting a school, but remember that you are an outside professional coming in to give the benefit of your experience and as such are entitled to your fee.

The fee for a single school visit, even if it's just for one hour with the children, will include time spent on:

- The initial enquiry.
- Subsequent emails or phone calls to confirm what will be involved.
- Preparation for the event or workshop.
- Travel to and from the school on the day, arriving half an hour early and allowing for traffic and/or public transport.
- With extra time ...
  - in case you get lost – schools can be amazingly difficult to find, particularly primary schools
  - because suddenly all the class want your autograph
  - to sign books if arrangements have been made with a local bookseller (or perhaps you have brought them to sell)
  - time spent with the local press
- Preparation of your invoice or filling in any other forms.

As a self-employed professional you are entitled to be paid for your time. If the school is far away, travel expenses may cover your monetary costs, but the time spent travelling is not covered. This is why many writers stipulate a larger fee if there is only one session and the school is some distance away, because the entire day is lost in travelling there and back.

If the school cannot afford two sessions, it's a good idea to suggest that they (or you) contact another local school or library so that they can share the travel expenses between them. That way everyone wins, and they see that you are making an effort to help minimise costs to make it more worthwhile for everyone.

The initial enquiry

It's essential to have down in writing EXACTLY what you expect to be doing. And agree it with the teacher beforehand. Otherwise you'll be open to the: 'Oh, the infants are so excited to have an author in school ... can you just come and read to them for 20 minutes?' syndrome. I'd advise no more than two sessions a day, or you can find yourself 'teaching' all seven periods.

Adele Geras

When someone calls or emails to ask you to visit, it's useful to have some kind of a checklist (perhaps at the front of your diary), so that you don't forget to ask any important questions. Find out the following:

- Agreed date and time of the visit.
- What class/age group they want you to speak to.
- How many children in each group.
- How long is a session? How many are you prepared to do/do they want?
- Times of sessions – are you happy with the amount of time in between?
- Directions to school and contact information and times, with any traffic/parking problems you might encounter at that time of day.
- Discussion of fees and method of payment. Try to arrange a cheque on the day, on presentation of your invoice.
- Travel and subsistence expenses. The current Inland Revenue mileage rates, allowable as deductible expenses for tax purposes when using your car for business purposes, are 40p per mile for the first 10,000 miles, 25p per mile after that (some organisations offer less).
- Any equipment you might need, i.e. flipchart, table, projector, etc.
- Bookselling arrangements – whether you bring books to sell or a local bookshop is contacted.
- Publicity. Ask if the school might like to contact the local press about your visit – good publicity for the school (and for you).

- Your cancellation fee (if they cancel less than a week ahead. This is not unreasonable; you may have refused another booking).
- Arrangements for refreshments, i.e. lunch, etc.
- Have the children read your book? Do they know who you are? Mention any preparation you would like *them* to do in advance of your visit.
- If the school has no idea what you do or about your books, you may want to ask why they approached you in particular (is it because they have a school inspection due and an author visit looks good?).
- Ask for a letter or email confirming the details of the visit, directions, contact details for the school and any arrangements, if you are being collected from public transport.
- Tell them a teacher must be present at all times because your insurance doesn't cover you if left alone in the class. If they ask about Disclosure (*see* below), tell them that this should not be an issue, as you will not be left alone with the children at any time.

If they have funding, find out if they require an invoice (this gives you the opportunity to ask if the cheque could be prepared beforehand so that you can take it away with you). Most authors will be Schedule D (self-employed) tax-payers, in which case the organiser should not be deducting tax or NI contributions from your fee. One way of making sure all this is agreed beforehand is to send off a letter to be signed by the organiser. Include the details of time and place and the sessions you have agreed to, together with the fee, adding something like this at the foot of the letter:

> '*Agreed dates can only be reserved for one week unless confirmation has been received. A cancellation fee of £50 is payable in the event of a cancellation by [the event organiser] five working days or less before the session date. This service is provided by a Schedule D tax-payer and it is therefore a booking condition that payment should be made in full, as per invoice, and that income tax, etc. should not be deducted at source.*'

Insurance

Public liability insurance is available for visiting writers; see the Society of Authors' Quick Guide to school visits, available free to members and for a small fee to non-members. Many schools and local authorities now insist that those visiting schools and libraries have some form of public liability insurance, as do other bodies. If a local authority insists on greater cover, the answer may be to charge the extra cost to the organisation.

Disclosure

'Schools and other organisers of events involving children and young adults increasingly insist on clearance from the Criminal Records Bureau, and we recommend ensuring that you have enhanced disclosure. In addition, insist that a teacher accompany you at all times, or your insurance will be invalidated. Databases such as NAWE's Artscape ask for evidence of an Enhanced Disclosure for working with children, and will help you process a Disclosure check via the CRB (Criminal Records Bureau).'
(Extract from Quick Guide, The Society of Authors)

You can contact the Criminal Records Bureau at this address: CRB Registration, PO Box 110, Liverpool, L69 3EF. Disclosure Application Line, 0870 9090 844, or check their website www.crb.gov.
Disclosure is being asked for more often these days, but in fact you should never be left on your own with the children. You are a visitor to the school; you are not there to be in charge of the children, nor to police their behaviour.

27.

Money Matters – Contracts and Royalties

For many children's writers, the harsh reality is that, contrary to public perception, they do not make a lot of money from their books. Going into schools and doing other kinds of author visits are a ways of increasing their income to allow them to continue writing. It is essential, then, that you are never shy about asking for proper payment or chasing up unpaid invoices. Always make sure your expenses are covered – not just the cost of petrol, but also wear and tear on your vehicle. The tax office recommendation is currently 40p/mile.

Unfortunately it's surprising how many people expect a writer to come and talk for free, even though they would be horrified if they were asked to do a day's work for nothing. Some people think that if you sell books after an event, what you earn from that should be your payment. They don't realise how little you are making from the sale of each book.

At times you may do something for free, but make sure it is your choice. Signings at bookshops are generally not paid, but if the shop is going to ask a school class in for the morning it may not be quite the same thing. In the end it is your business what you charge and how rigidly you enforce it, but make sure that people do not try to take advantage of your good nature.

Contracts and royalties

Publishers' contracts are fairly long and complicated legal papers, so this is just an overview of some of the things you may encounter. Once the contract arrives you should have it checked over, by your agent if you have one. Alternatively you could consider joining the Society of Authors who will look over it and make suggestions. If you join as an associate member they will also look at your contracts with agents or publishers before you sign them, and give you advice on how to proceed.

Your editor will probably tell you that it is their 'standard' contract, but in fact contracts are pretty much up for negotiation on most points. The trick is to know what is worth fighting for and what is in fact an industry norm. Your publisher is generally not trying to 'do you out' of anything, but it is in their interests to get the best deal they can – and it is in yours to do the same for yourself.

Always ask for clarification if you are uncomfortable with any of the terms; it may be something that can be changed. Once you have signed a contract you are committed to its terms, so pay attention to what it says.

If you have not already finished the book there will be details such as delivery dates, possibly the length or word count, and any illustrations to agree on. The contract will also ask you to confirm that it is your original work and not infringing anyone's copyright, or containing any advice that might be dangerous, etc. There will be clauses regarding film, television and dramatic rights and almost any other rights you may or may not imagine. In fact, contracts seem to be getting longer all the time as new items are added to them.

Moral rights and copyright are asserted in the contract and will be printed in the book as stated. Avoid giving away your copyright: you automatically have copyright in anything you write for your lifetime and for 70 years after your death, unless you give it away in a contract.

Often the publisher will ask for first refusal on the author's next book. They then have to accept or refuse this within a stated amount of time after you have submitted it to them.

The contract will state the advance and royalty, or fee you are being offered. The advance is normally a non-returnable payment made before the book is published. The author earns no more from the book until the royalties due to them have exceeded the amount of the advance. It is worth trying to get a rising royalty, which means that once a certain number of books have been sold, the royalty rises by a few per cent. By then the publisher has recouped the initial production costs and a rising royalty means that the author also benefits at this time. A fee is a one-off payment, which means that regardless of how many books are sold it is all you will be paid for that book.

You, or your agent if you have one, may also be able to negotiate a larger royalty percentage, advance or fee, or alter the balance of when the payment is made – perhaps getting you more on signature of contract and less at publication or delivery. Your agent may also want to handle foreign rights for your book, although some publishers prefer to hold on to these rights so that they can handle the sale of them, particularly when it comes to picture books. Electronic Rights is another area that seems to be changing year on year as technology grows, which is why expert advice is especially helpful.

After you have signed and exchanged contracts with a publisher, they will send you a royalty statement every six months showing what has been sold, how much for and what your percentage is. They then deduct any advance you have been paid, after which any resulting money comes to you. You may never 'earn out' your advance (this simply means the book has earned, in royalties, the full amount of the initial advance), but it is yours to keep regardless of how many or how few books are sold, even if the book goes out of print before this happens.

If you have an agent they will receive any advances/royalties from your publisher and, after deducting their percentage and VAT, they should send the balance to you within a reasonably short space of time.

Most publishers' contracts state that royalties should be paid within three months of the end of the royalty period, often calculated from January to June and July to December, which means your royalties will be paid three months after that, in September and March.

Being self-employed

Many writers are so busy with the creative side of writing that they leave the business part of the job until it cries out for notice. For some, the desperate urge to write their book and get it published has taken all their attention and they have little or no interest in keeping accounts until it's forced onto them.

Unfortunately, this is the road to disaster. I can fully understand the irritation, but there is a tremendous amount of paperwork involved in writing, dealing with publishers, contracts, author visits, tax and all the rest. When the euphoria of getting published is over, you do need to look seriously at how you are going to keep your writing accounts, tax matters and so on in order. And, as with any small business, you need to be aware of the need to promote yourself and your books.

Obviously not everything needs to happen at once, and you may not earn enough from your writing to pay tax at all for a while, but you do need to keep all your receipts and invoices. If your book suddenly goes stellar you may need to register for VAT and you can then claim back the VAT on any writing-related VAT invoices you have paid in the previous three years. So it is well worth keeping hold of them, just in case!

Tax and accounting

Keeping good, clear accounts makes everyone's life easier in the long run, even if you hate all that (and lots of people do). Try not to ignore it, because it just won't go away. Unfortunately the truth is that as soon as you start earning reasonable money and are getting really busy with little time to call your own, that is when it can become overwhelming. You will be grateful for a little thought and organisation at the beginning; it will save you money and time if you try not to throw everything into a shoebox and ignore it.

One of the difficulties of being a writer is that your income is unpredictable. It will depend on how well your books sell; this is an unknown quantity until your royalty statements come in every six months or so. Income can vary tremendously and when the letter drops through your door it may be a lovely surprise or a depressing reality-check, but you will have little or no warning of what to expect.

Your income will also depend on whether your next book has been accepted, thus generating another advance or fee, and also on how many school or library visits or writing residencies you are offered or are able to take on. These need to be organised carefully so that time is ring-fenced for writing. Your variable income makes it very difficult to plan and causes a lot of highs and lows emotionally, but it is another reason to keep your accounts carefully so that you can track what is due to come in.

Keep an eye on your royalty statements and don't imagine that your agent or publisher is handling all that so you don't need to bother about it. It is no different from checking your change when you buy a bottle of milk. People make mistakes and miss things, but it's your income – it's up to you to make sure it's right.

If you become self-employed as a writer you need to register this fact with your local tax office. If you are unsure, a quick call to check with them can save you a lot of trouble later. If you are writing as an extra and have another income, you need to fill your writing income and expenses in on that part of your tax return. Again, the tax office will advise you on this.

You can set up a simple filing system for your writing affairs, divided into legal contracts and agreements; royalty statements; invoices you send out for author visits; invoices you pay for any book stock you buy from your publisher; and receipts for stationery, computer supplies, etc. I find it useful to keep a separate diary for writing and for author visits. This is a good way of checking you have got everything straight in your accounts and keeps the details all in one place.

You can also set up a simple accounting system, either on a computer spreadsheet or just in a book with columns. You will need to note your income on one side and your expenditure on another. It is useful to have a separate bank account for your writing earnings.

Your income sheet should show any income you have that is

related to your writing; this might include payments of royalties, advances, PLR and ALCS (*see* below), author visit fees, books you sell, date, payee, type of payment and so on. Your outgoing sheet should be the same. Some of the things to put on this might include: stationery, computer supplies, email, website and broadband payments; research costs and expenses; books bought for reference or from your publisher for resale; petrol and parking – where it relates to your writing; meetings with publishers or agent; research; National Insurance payments; and bank charges.

All earnings and expenses related to writing need to be calculated and entered into your tax return. You can also include a percentage of tax relief for use of certain items, e.g. your car (if applicable), landline and mobile phone. You can claim for the use of part of your home, if that is where you work; this can include everything from a percentage of mortgage and heating payments to computer and other equipment and furniture. Here it is important to make sure you get good professional advice, as there can be other tax implications to claiming sole use of even a single room in the house. It is often better to work out a percentage of the use of parts of your home and household bills for writing, but an accountant can help you get this right. The Society of Authors also has a Quick Guide on tax for writers, available free to members and at a small cost for non-members.

Travel and other expenses incurred in research can be legitimately claimed against tax, but remember that you can only claim back your expenses if you are earning enough from writing to pay tax. You can find out about how to calculate this yourself, but I would advise that if you become self-employed or if your writing income looks like being a reasonable amount, you get some quotes from an accountant for their services, – one who knows about writers and their earnings. Their expertise can save you a lot of time and money because they will know what you can claim and how to do it.

If you get paid in any foreign currency, take a note of the exchange rate when the payment is made so that if it changes either up or down, you or your accountant can make allowances on your tax return.

There are a few other things worth mentioning, such as VAT. If your earnings exceed the annual amount stipulated in any 12-month period, you are obliged to register for VAT and make payments of 17.5% of any earnings. You can set against this any VAT paid on writing-related goods or services as long as you have VAT receipts; this includes fuel. You will, if you become VAT registered, have to charge VAT on any invoices you send out and notify your publishers. All the information can be obtained from www.vatcentre.com or the HM Revenue office.

Some other income for authors

PLR – Public Lending Right
This is the payment that you get when your book is borrowed from public libraries. You are required to register your book for PLR. The payment year runs from 30th June each year, so if you register your book before that you will be sent a statement the following January. To qualify you have to be named on the title page or be entitled to a royalty from the publisher. You may also have to share PLR with any illustrator or co-author on a basis of percentage share. All the details and registration information is on the PLR website www.plr.uk.com, which is easy to use and understand.

ALCS – Author's Licensing and Collecting Society
They protect the rights of all UK writers and ensure that they are 'fairly compensated for any works that are copied, broadcast or recorded'. They also collect and distribute this money to authors. More information is available on their website www.alcs.co.uk. All members of the Society of Authors or the Writer's Guild are entitled to free membership of ALCS; other writers can pay a one-off membership fee of £25.

This fee and any other professional organisation fees (such as membership of the Society of Authors) should be noted down and are all tax-deductible, as is your accountant's fee. Having an accountant can be very useful and if you do pay tax, they can sometimes save you as much as their fee by giving you good advice. If you are looking for an accountant, ask around and try to get one who has experience working with writers.

A good children's story has something in common with a good sonnet, in that it forces you to compress and distil all you want to say. Writing for children is challenging, rewarding, and I've never really wanted to do anything else.

Kate Langrish

Section 5
Useful Information

Glossary of Terms

Advance This is an 'advance on royalties'; a non-returnable sum paid to the author before the book has earned any royalties. The author earns no further money until the royalties exceed the amount paid as an advance.

Blurb The short description of a book usually found on the back cover to entice the reader to buy or read the book. Not to be confused with a **synopsis**.

Co-edition Where a book is sold to more than one publisher in different countries.

Disclosure or **Enhanced Disclosure** Clearance obtained from the Criminal Records Bureau to enable you to work with children.

Double-Page Spread Two facing pages of an illustrated book.

Edition When a new edition of a book is produced, it is different in some way from the last. It is not just a reprint.

Fee A one-off payment, paid instead of royalties.

Impression This is when the book is reprinted – more copies are printed with no changes.

Imprint Some publishers publish different kinds of books under different brand names. These are called imprints.

Imprint page (copyright page) The page with the publisher's details, the copyright sign with author's name and date, the ISBN number and any other relevant details.

ISBN International Standard Book Number. This is the 10- or 13-digit number you find on the **imprint page** and usually on the back cover of a book.

List A publisher's list is all the books that the publisher produces. Publishers use their list as a form of branding, with their own style of books and authors.

PLR Public Lending Right is the payment you get when your book is borrowed from a library. A rotating selection of libraries is used to collect the PLR data to ensure fairness. Authors have to register their books for PLR.

Publishing:
- **Trade Publishers** Publish books to be sold by bookshops/ Internet stores, to the general public.
- **Educational Publishers** Publish books sold primarily into schools for use by teachers as teaching materials.
- **Vanity Publishing** When you pay to get your book published regardless of its merit. There is usually little or no editorial or marketing involved.
- **Self-publishing** Where you become the publisher and handle all aspects of publishing yourself.
- **Print on Demand** Where new copies of a book are printed only after an order has been received for them.

Royalty A percentage of the price of a book, which is paid to the author by the publisher.

Synopsis A complete summary of your plot, leaving no questions unanswered.

Contributing Writers

My thanks to the talented writers and publishing professionals who have contributed to this book. You will find information about most of the children's writers listed below on the SAS (Scattered Authors Society) website, www.scatteredauthors.org.

Jenny Alexander
Lynne Benton
Julie Bertagna
Alan Cliff
Penny Dolan
Fiona Dunbar
Malachy Doyle
Terry Edge
Vivian French
Adele Geras
Pippa Goodhart
Nick Green
Griselda Gifford
Diana Hendry
Mary Hoffman
Julia Jarman
Cindy Jefferies
Catherine Johnson
Eizabeth Kay
Joanna Kenrick
Kate Langrish
Joan Lennon

Joan Lingard
Rebecca Lisle
Catherine MacPhail
Nicola Morgan
Caroline Pitcher
Sue Purkiss
Celia Rees
Mark Robson
Stewart Ross
Helen Salter
Eleanor Updale
Valerie Wilding
Jeanne Willis
Liz Niven (Poet)
Brenda Stones (freelance
    editor and writer)
Mary Hamley (Senior Editor,
    Pearson Education)

Also quoted:
Isaac Asimov
Anton Chekov

Organisations and Associations for Writers

The Society of Authors
(also The Society of Authors in Scotland)
84 Drayton Gardens, London SW10 9SB
www.societyofauthors.org

The Writers' Guild of Great Britain
15 Britannia Street, London WC1X 9JN
www.writersguild.org.uk

The Scattered Authors Society (SAS)
Membership open to all published writers for young people.
www.scatteredauthors.org

Arts Council England
14 Great Peter Street, London SW1P 3NQ
www.artscouncil.org.uk

Scottish Arts Council
12 Manor Place, Edinburgh EH3 7DD
www.scottisharts.org.uk

Booktrust
Book House, 45 East Hill, London SW18 2QZ
www.booktrust.org.uk

Scottish Book Trust (Live Literature Funding)
Sandeman House, Trunk's Close, 55 High Street,
Edinburgh EH1 1SR
www.scottishbooktrust.com

Federation of Children's Book Groups
Information about The Book Trust and the annual Children's
Book award.
www.fcbg.org.uk

The Poetry Library
Level 5, Royal Festival Hall, London SE1 8XX
www.poetrylibrary.org.uk

Scottish Poetry Library
Crichton's Close, Canongate, Edinburgh EH8 8DT
www.spl.org.uk

Edinburgh L'Unesco City of Literature
www.cityofliterature.com

National Association of Writers in Education (NAWE)
PO Box 1, Sheriff Hutton, York YO6 7YU
www.nawe.co.uk

PLR – Public Lending Right
www.plr.uk.com

ALCS – Authors' Licensing and Collecting Agency
www.alcs.co.uk

Literaturetraining.com
Information on a wide variety of items relating to writing and
literature.
www.literaturetraining.com

Writernet
The Playwrights Network
www.writernet.org.uk

Writing Courses and Literary Consultancies

Writing courses:

Arvon Foundation
Residential writing courses.
www.arvonfoundation.org

Literary consultancies:

Cornerstones
www.cornerstones.co.uk

The Literary Consultancy
www.literaryconsultancy.co.uk

Writers' Ark
www.thewritersark.co.uk

The Writers' Workshop
www.writersworkshop.co.uk

Magazines and Websites

Achuka
www.achuka.co.uk

Armadillo
www.armadillomagazine.com

BBC website
Writing for film, TV, radio and theatre.
www.bbc.co.uk/writersroom

Book2Book
www.booktrade.info

Books for Keeps
www.booksforkeeps.co.uk

Carousel
www.carouselguide.co.uk

Contact an Author
A searchable database for contacting authors for events, etc.
www.contactanauthor.co.uk

Readingzone
www.readingzone.com

Wordpool
Children's book site for parents, teachers and writers.
www.wordpool.co.uk

Write Away
www.writeaway.org.uk

Writers' News
www.writersnews.co.uk

A Writer's Bookshelf

An Author's Guide to Publishing *Michael Legat* (Hale, 1982)
Children's Writers' & Artists' Yearbook (A&C Black)
From Pitch to Publication *Carole Blake* (Pan Books, 1999)
Marketing Your Book *Alison Baverstock* (A&C Black)
Our Thoughts Are Bees: writers working with schools *Mandy Coe and Jean Sprackland* (Wordplay Press, 2005)
The Writer's Craft (creative writing in schools) *Valerie Thornton* (Hodder Gibson, 2006)
Writer's Handbook Guide to Writing for Children (Macmillan)
Writing Poetry *Doris Corti* (Thomas & Lochar, 1994)

Inspirational books for writers:

A Room of One's Own *Virginia Woolf* (Penguin)
Becoming a Writer *Dorothea Brande* (Macmillan)
On Writing *Stephen King* (Hodder and Stoughton)

Notes on Publishers' Guidelines

Most publishers suggest that their lists nowadays are predominantly author-led – meaning that the stories presented to them by authors are judged individually rather than being set in specific series. Much will depend on the story, the language, and the style, which will combine to dictate the desired length of the book, and what age of child it will best suit.

Age ranges as given below and elsewhere in this book are loose classifications, intended merely to give some guidelines. As all children are different and have widely varied abilities, interests and levels of emotional development, 'books for children' cannot be accurately classified by age.

Here are a few examples, giving suggested word counts and age ranges for titles or series that are available as this book goes to print. As with any list of this kind, the information is likely to become out of date very quickly, so readers are advised to check directly with the publisher before making an approach.

Picture books
Generally full-colour illustrations; mainly author-led; generally under 1000 words.

For young readers aged approximately 5–7 years
Illustrations vary between colour and b/w line drawings.

Some examples:

A & C Black (Publishers) Ltd:
5–7 yrs – **Chameleons,** approximately 1200 to 1400 words
6–7 yrs (KS1) – **White Wolves,** 500, 900 and 1400 words

Penguin Books/Puffin:
5 yrs+ – **Colour Young Puffins,** approximately 2000 words

Anderson Press:
5–8 yrs (early readers; fiction) – approximately 3000 to 5000 words

Macmillan:
5–7 yrs (young fiction) – approximately 3000 words

Egmont:
4–5 yrs – **Green Bananas,** approximately 500 words
5–6 yrs – **Blue Bananas,** approximately 1000 words
6 yrs – **Red Bananas,** approximately 2000 words

For older readers
7–12 yrs – generally varying between 15,000 and 50,000 words; mainly author-led.

A Final Word

Writing for children is challenging, exciting and never dull, and I feel privileged to be able to spend my time doing something I love.

One of my reasons for wanting to write this book was that when running writing workshops and giving talks to aspiring writers, I have seen how confusing the world of writing and publishing can be for those wishing to enter it for the first time – and even for those whose first book is just out, all new and shiny.

There are so many different paths you can take, and one of the things I enjoy most is the fact that one day I might be working on a picture book and the next on a novel. I wanted to give some idea of the reality behind the expectations and media hype that surrounds writing and writers, at the same time as helping and encouraging those who specifically want to write for children.

A childhood friend used to tell wonderful stories. I was envious of her ability to think up these stories because I knew I had no imagination; I had it on good authority – when I was eight years old a teacher had written 'this child lacks imagination' on my report card. This stayed with me for many years and although it never stopped me loving books and stories, perhaps for many years it prevented my even considering that I might be a writer myself. Everyone has imagination and sometimes it only needs permission to come out and play!

I would like to thank all the great children's writers who have contributed to this book and particularly the wonderful Scattered Authors Society – a warm and generous band of writers. My thanks also to the other publishing professionals who have taken time from their busy schedules to answer my queries, and to Katie Taylor and Hilary Lissenden and everyone at A &C Black.

As always I am indebted to my agent Kathryn Ross and also to Lindsey Fraser, at Fraser Ross Associates, for their support – and to my long-suffering husband, Stuart, our children and their partners, for their forbearance and supplies of chocolate!

Linda Strachan, July 2008

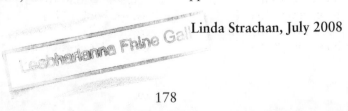

Index